The Euro

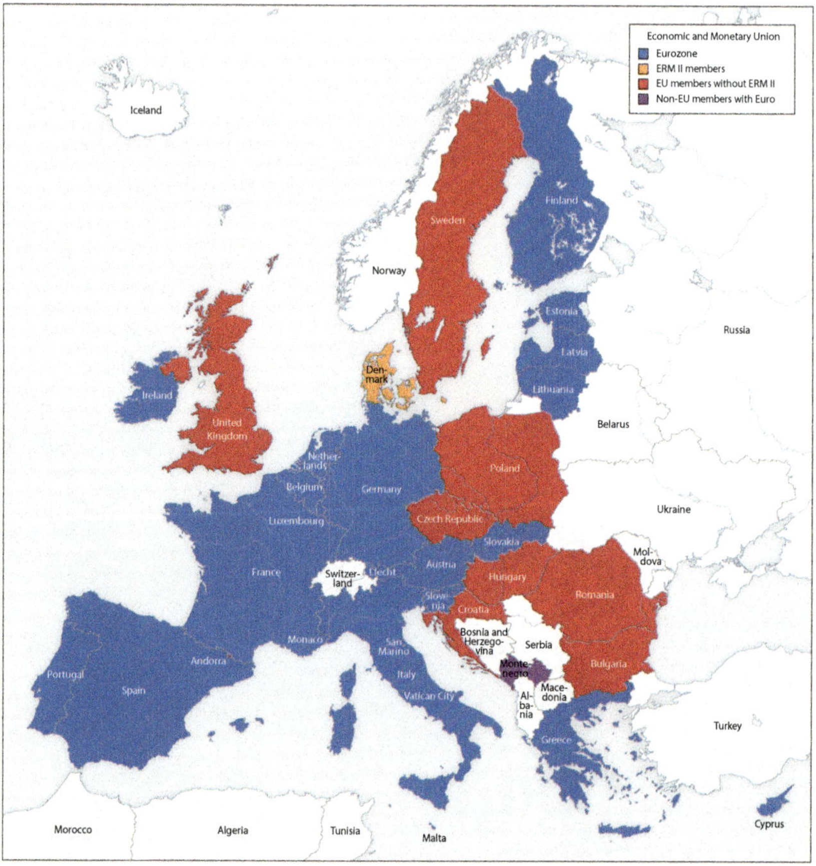

EU and the Eurozone (Map)

Jesper Jespersen

The Euro

Why it Failed

palgrave
macmillan

Jesper Jespersen
Roskilde University
Roskilde, Denmark

ISBN 978-3-319-46387-2 ISBN 978-3-319-46388-9 (eBook)
DOI 10.1007/978-3-319-46388-9

Library of Congress Control Number: 2016951679

Printed on acid-free paper

This Palgrave Macmillan imprint is published by Springer Nature
The registered company is Springer International Publishing AG
The registered company address is: Gewerbestrasse 11, 6330 Cham, Switzerland

Preface

I have worked on European monetary integration ever since I wrote my PhD dissertation on 'Theories of Balance of Payments with special regard to the Danish Capital Account', which was defended in September 1979 at the European University Institute (EUI), Florence, Italy. Since then, it has been a dramatic period in the history of European macroeconomic development. I have followed it closely and have taken an active part in debates leading up to the two referenda we have had in Denmark on the participation in the European Monetary Union in the years 1992 and 2000. Each time the proposal was rejected, a majority of voters did not find the arguments of giving up monetary sovereignty in favour of an uncertain act of European integration, although the positive economic arguments at that time were presented by the experts as pretty undisputable.

The title of the book is referring to the mismatch between the prosperous prospects, which supported the introduction of the euro, and the devastating macroeconomic realities, which later met a number of Euro countries. So, in many ways it is rather the economic arguments that failed. The institutional framework surrounding the Euro could not overcome the challenges related to the introduction of the common currency. To the contrary, it will be argued in the book, this framework was derived from a misleading and unrealistic macroeconomic theory. Therefore, the Euro failed in its present form. What the future will bring is impossible to say. It is a matter of political aspiration, ideology, democratic processes and an, hopefully, improved understanding of the working of European macroeconomic and monetary reality.

During the years, I have benefitted a lot from research, supervision and teaching at the EUI, at Copenhagen University and for the last 20 years at Roskilde University, Denmark. In addition, I have deepened my understanding from being a research fellow in Cambridge, UK, and Dijon, France. The importance of Professor Niels Thygesen, University of Copenhagen, as a continued source of respectful inspiration cannot be exaggerated. In addition, I would like to thank my colleague Bruno Amoroso for a countless number of conversations on Southern Europe and Scandinavia – how can they be so different in many respects? Practical matters could not have been solved without the efficient help from Daniel Rayburn (language) and Henrik Jensen (figures). Finally, I have got financial support from Otto Bruun's Fond, which is highly appreciated.

Copenhagen, Denmark
July 2016

Jesper Jespersen

Contents

List of Figures

List of Tables

List of Boxes

CHAPTER 1

Eurozone Crises

Abstract The Eurozone countries have experienced historic macroeconomic imbalances measured by unemployment and balance-of-payments deficits and surpluses. At the same time, Eurozone countries have been following diverging macroeconomic courses since the financial crisis of 2008. Some countries are still suffering from a stagnating or even lower GDP than 10 years ago, whereas other Euro countries have grown faster than pre-2008 while at the same time reducing unemployment. On average, however, the Eurozone economy has performed significantly weaker than the non-euro economies in the EU, mainly due to a misperceived iron law of required fiscal budget balance by the member countries. The policies pursued by Eurozone institutions have been guided by misunderstood macroeconomic principles.

Keywords Broken Euro-promises · Historical high unemployment · Increasing macroeconomic imbalances · Beggar-thou-neighbour wages policies · Iron law of fiscal budget balance

The introduction of the euro has had profound consequences for the economies of Europe. Why the introduction of the euro has caused such a widespread economic distress has hardly been recognised in macroeconomic textbooks or by policy makers within the EU system. The gravest consequences have been for the European Monetary Union (EMU) although, since 2010, the negative impact of monetary union has depressed the European Union (EU) as a whole. However, a genuine

J. Jespersen, *The Euro*, DOI 10.1007/978-3-319-46388-9_1

catastrophe has befallen those countries in the Eurozone, which experienced a substantial balance-of-payments deficit and accumulating foreign debt in the years leading up to the financial crisis of 2008. Suddenly they found themselves in a money trap without access to liquidity. They realised the hard way that they had lost their monetary and financial sovereignty.

These Eurozone countries are still far below their previous level of GDP and have experienced an unbearably high rate of unemployment and social stress.

The symptoms of the economic disease of a malfunctioning monetary union are straightforward to diagnose. Stagnating production and increased unemployment in the Eurozone are to be considered as problems affecting the EU as a whole. However, within the Eurozone, these developments have been very unevenly distributed. Those countries with a weak balance of payments – Greece, Spain, Portugal and Cypress – have experienced a steep rise in unemployment. In contrast, Germany, Austria and the Netherlands have, together with a number of non-Euro countries, seen a fall in unemployment and reasonable growth rates after 2010.

Official explanations as to why southern European countries have failed primarily point to public sector deficits and debt, together with inflexible labour markets. EU economists in and around Brussels (and Berlin), which Chap. 2 will characterise more precisely, have largely discarded factors not related to public sector finances as the main reasons for macroeconomic imbalances. When the institutional working rules of the Eurozone were established, the focus was confined to public finances. The so-called Growth and Stability Pact agreed in 1996 focused on public sector deficits as the only major obstacle to a well-functioning European Monetary Union. Upon the advice of EU economists, the European Council decided that public deficits should never exceed 3 per cent of GDP, except in the unlikely case of recession. However, no one could explain where this number – 3 per cent of GDP – came from. Furthermore, no one could explain convincingly why it should be the same for all EU countries, particularly if one considers the eye-catching structural as well as welfare state differences that exist between the EU countries.

On the contrary, not a single word was mentioned in the institutional framework with regard to putting a limit to balance-of-payments imbalances, not even in the macroeconomic convergence criteria which countries have had to fulfil in order to become members of the Eurozone. Quite the opposite, EU economists argued that when Eurozone countries adopt the same currency, the balance-of-payments problem would cease to be a macroeconomic problem. Reality has demonstrated that they were entirely wrong. However, it is a fact which is still waiting to be recognised in textbooks giving the theoretical foundation of the European Monetary Union, see for instance De Grauwe (11th ed.) (2016). From their perspective, it is still mainly a matter of balancing the public sector and setting up a federal political structure. They do not accept balance-of-payments imbalances caused by the premature introduction of the euro as causing high unemployment, stagnating European economy and hereby increased pressures on public finance. In most textbooks, unemployment is caused mainly, if not solely, by the lack of labour market flexibility (i.e. money wages and/or migration). In fact, public sector welfare expenses are seen as obstructions to much needed and necessary labour market adjustments in countries with high unemployment.

This book is concerned with real-world economic problems; notably, problems in the Eurozone that arise when politicians are advised (and misled) by economists, who work with macroeconomic theories and models which are detached from reality. In addition, some of these economists do distrust the ability of the democratic political system to make 'prudent' decisions, owing to politicians' short-sightedness and emphasis on their re-election rather than undertaking responsibility for the process of European integration. Without hesitation, these economists have recommended that, for instance, the board of directors of the European Central Bank should be absolutely independent of the political system. They also fully supported the request of Greece and Italy to be governed, for a while, by a technocrat government headed by a former EU economist (Fig. 1.1).

In this book, in order to demonstrate how and why the Eurozone is in disarray, I look more closely at the Eurozone as a whole and compare its macroeconomic developments with developments in EU countries that have kept their own currency. In addition, I take a closer look at the development within the Eurozone with a main focus on the four largest countries: Germany, France, Italy and Spain. My plan here is to demonstrate that, first, the Eurozone is not in any reasonable understanding of the words an *Optimal Currency Area*, which has created tensions among the member states, and second, that policy

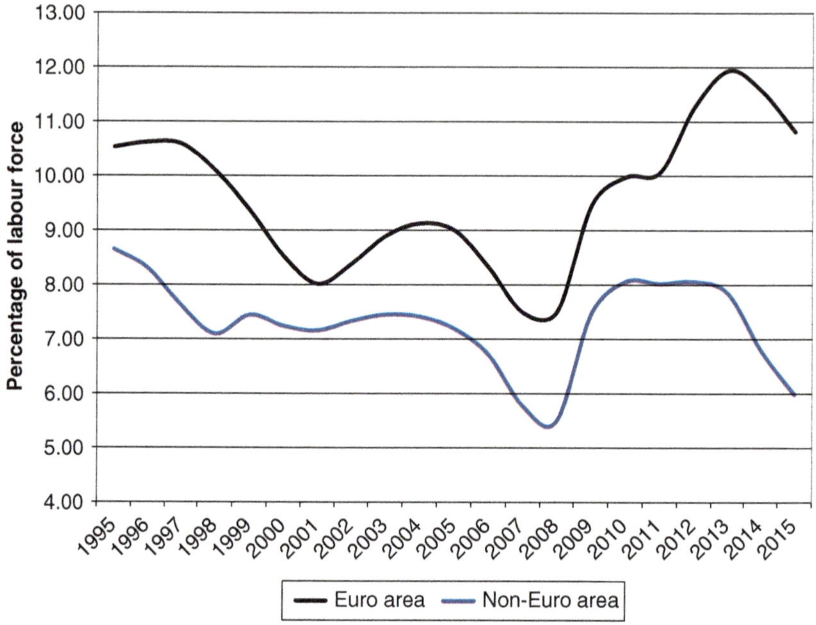

Fig. 1.1 Unemployment within and outside the Eurozone

Note: Non-euro countries consist of UK, Sweden, Poland and the Czech Republic
Source: OECD, Economic Outlook, 2016 and own calculation

recommendations and request by creditors have enlarged the intra-Eurozone macroeconomic imbalances at a scale which is without any historical precedent over the past 70 years.

Hence, I intend to demonstrate how doubtful many of the high-profile macroeconomic diagnoses have proved to having been derived from an unrealistic economic theory which recommends a sole focus on public sector deficit in order to re-balance the Eurozone. By disregarding other important macroeconomic imbalances and policy instruments outside their policy concern and recommendations, EU economists have derailed the entire Eurozone project to such an extent that the Eurozone itself has been at risk of falling apart. This possibility of collapse was, indeed, openly discussed over the summer of 2015, although it was pushed aside by the Greek government submitting to the requirements of EU economists headed by the EU Commission, the ECB and the IMF.

Until 2007, Spain had a balanced budget and even a surplus for a few years, whereas Germany had considerable deficits, which even exceeded the EU-imposed limit of 3 percent of GDP. Germany was then asked by the EU Commission to save on public finances even though the rate of unemployment was close to 10 percent just after the turn of the century. In contrast, Spain was growing quite fast as a consequence of a low level of interest and a private sector building boom. Spain was praised and Germany blamed, whereas the opposite should have been the case considering that when the financial crisis hit Spain, the housing bubble burst and private banks were brought to or beyond the brink of bankruptcy. Moreover, unemployment rose steeply and public finances were burdened by huge social expenditures and a number of bank rescue packages. On the other hand, Germany has benefited from having had the lowest wage inflation amongst all the Eurozone countries for several years, which has made a significant contribution to Germany's international competitiveness, particularly in terms of boosting exports to the other Euro countries and to the emerging economies.

In the years leading up to the crisis, Germany was therefore becoming the heavyweight within the Eurozone. Nonetheless, within a few years, the German government's budget deficit was at stake in contravening the 3 percent budget rule of the Stability Pact. Instead of realising that the institutional set-up was wanting and countries were still divergent, the German chancellor just begged for a special case exemption from the European Council. At the same time, the Spanish economy was heading along at relatively high growth rates, with expanding employment caused by a private sector building boom and a growing balance-of-payments deficit. However, the EU economists did not care about these private sector imbalances as long as the public sector budget was balanced. On the contrary, Spain was used as an example to demonstrate the positive impact of introducing the euro and an argument for more EU countries to join the Eurozone. However, when the crisis hit in 2008, Spain was much harder hit by the crisis in terms of rising unemployment due to the huge balance-of-payments deficits and foreign debt, which could not be financed.

The important role of the balance of payments for macroeconomic stability is the main concern of this book. The difference in development after 2008 between the two just-mentioned countries shows how misleading this blinkered focus on public sector budgets has proved to be with regard to understanding the real underlying macroeconomic imbalances that reduce countries' resilience when a crisis hits (Fig. 1.2).

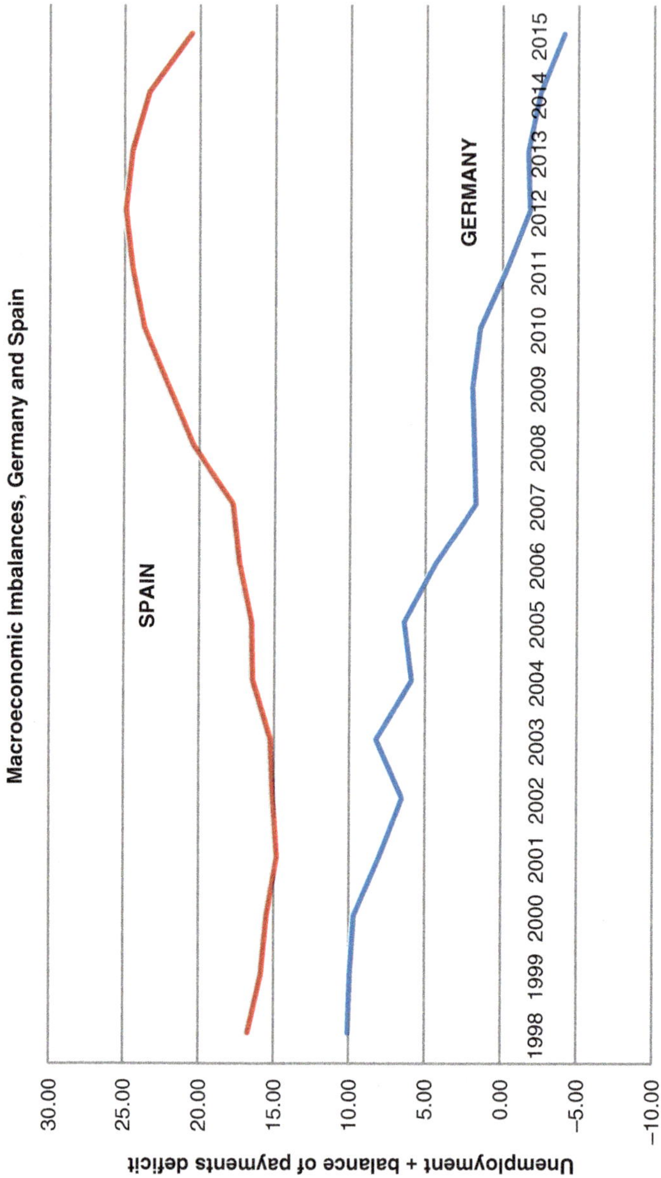

Fig. 1.2 Macroeconomic imbalance, Germany and Spain

Source: Own calculation using OECD, Economic Outlook, June 2016, Data

Why has the Euro failed? The answers are manifold and provide the main content of this book. Of course, there is no single answer; I should rather say that the failure is the sum of a number of misguided decisions initiated by a group of politicians, economists and civil servants close to Brussels during the 1990s and early 2000s when European integration and de-regulation of the national and European economies were high on the political agenda. The fall of the Berlin Wall and the Iron Curtain in Europe gave strong political and ideological momentum to neoliberalism and European market integration. The phrases *More Europe* and *More market* became more or less synonymous. Here, one (European) currency came to be seen as an instrument to promote both ideas. Hence, the next step in the message coming from Brussels was to proclaim *One Market, One Money* – which sounded almost trivial. The populist argument is that you save exchange costs when travelling or trading across borders and a common currency makes it easier to compare prices within Europe. Both arguments are of course true, but it is a fact you don't need a university degree in economics to understand, and only represent a small part of the larger picture. So, if the macroeconomic consequences are left aside, then the presentation is lopsided.

The macroeconomic arguments have unquestionably become the most pressing; but they are also, admittedly, the most difficult to understand and explain unless you argue from a general equilibrium perspective. Realist macroeconomics arguments have to address the characteristics of the economic structures and traditions of the participation economies with regard to welfare state, productivity, labour market organisations and banking and financial sectors. What does it mean to give up important national policy instruments when the macroeconomic future is uncertain and the adjustments pattern to external (and internal) shocks are quite different? And what happens if there is no formal agreement among the participation countries within the Eurozone to support each other when countries are hit differently and yet they have accepted giving up their national money, their specific exchange rate, and have to adjust to strict limits to the public sector budget, that is, fiscal policy? These questions posed by realist macroeconomists were, unfortunately, not addressed when the EMU was designed.

However, expectations were high in the wake of the fall of the Berlin Wall, and the Euro was presented as one more step in the inevitable movement towards an 'ever closer union' bringing prosperity to all Europeans. This has evidently not happened. Expectations were not fulfilled and an increasing number of Europeans are today becoming sceptical towards the European project in the present form without prosperity.

This book explains why the monetary union, the stability pact and the euro together have caught a number of Euro countries in a macroeconomic trap causing a social collapse, which the hardest hit countries cannot get out of by their own means. They are no longer in command of their own economic destiny.

Accordingly, it is hardly an exaggeration to claim that the euro has failed. It might not disappear entirely. The future of the euro will be decided in Berlin and Brussels, in what form no one can say today, but hopefully through a more democratic process than hitherto and with the guidance of euro-realists to prevent the EU from falling apart.

CHAPTER 2

'Optimal' Currency Area: What Does It Mean?

Abstract The original theory of an 'Optimal Currency Area' was presented by Mundell (A theory of optimal currency areas. Am Econ Rev 51: 657–665, 1961). Conclusions were drawn using a neoclassical general equilibrium framework. This theory was employed when the Euro-monetarists, dominating the Delors-Commission (Report on economic and monetary union in the European community, Office for Official Publications of the EC, Luxemburg, 1989), recommended the establishment of a European Monetary Union, an independent European Central Bank, defined convergence criteria and the rules of public sector balanced budget. The theory has failed to foresee the current Euro crises. Alternatively, Euro-realistic theory, which takes analytical inspiration from Keynes's macroeconomic methodology by using consistent stock-flow modelling, would have led to other and much less optimistic conclusions with regard to the outcome of imposing a common currency on the EU countries.

Keywords Dividing macroeconomic theories · Euro-monetarists · Euro-realists · Misunderstood theory of 'Optimal Currency Area' · Persistent imbalances

Introduction

It is not an easy task to evaluate the economic consequences of joining a monetary union. It is a decision that involves renouncing not only the national currency but also a collection of related policy instruments.

J. Jespersen, *The Euro*, DOI 10.1007/978-3-319-46388-9_2

Hence, the outcome of such an evaluation depends heavily on the theoretical framework used for the analysis.

The chapter presents two different schools of macroeconomic thought: *neoclassical monetarism* and *Keynes(ian) realism*.

The monetarist school takes inspiration from Robert Mundell's groundbreaking paper, written in 1961, in which the concept of an optimal currency area was originally presented. Here, permanent microeconomic benefits (reduced transaction costs) are evaluated in relation to the transitory macroeconomic cost (the loss of output during the transition to full employment).

Keynes-inspired macroeconomists doubt if such a mechanical benefit and cost calculation can be undertaken due to the lack of knowledge regarding the adjustment mechanisms within the macroeconomic system and due to fundamental uncertainty about future events. Hence, within this more realistic analytical framework, macroeconomic costs are caused by a persistent balance-of-payments deficit, unemployment, loss of output and debt accumulation. Without a federal political structure, it is then difficult to see how benefits should outweigh the costs of losing important policy instruments, such as monetary and exchange change rate policies, as well as a limited use of fiscal policy.

A Euro Is Not Just a Means of Payment

We could imagine a single household or a firm posing the hypothetical question: why has the EU *not* introduced a common currency to avoid money transaction costs for tourists and to promote trade and financial capital flows across borders all over the common European market?

From an individual point of view, the above statement makes absolute sense. One has to be a trained macroeconomist to understand that money is not just a neutral means of transaction, which can then be made into a common unit of accounting to facilitate trade and travel domestically and internationally. As we shall discuss later, the macroeconomic consequences of adopting a common currency differ markedly between participating countries.

As a unit of accounting, a means of payment and a store of value, money has a number of derived implications, which differ from country to country. These differences therefore make the construction of a monetary union independent from the adoption of, for instance, the same metric system, that is, where a kilometre is a kilometre regardless of which country you travel through.

As we shall see, a 'Euro' is not always a 'Euro' independent of the Euro country in which one lives. The real value of a euro is lower in countries with a high level of prices. The higher the level of price anwd costs, the fewer goods and services one can buy. Furthermore, when we consider the impact of 'Euros', we should separate the quality of the euro currency issued by the European Central Bank (ECB) and the Euros issued as deposits in private banks. A euro-note can be used as a means of payments all over the Euro-area.

However, the quality, or general acceptance, of a euro deposit in a private bank depends on the reputation of the bank and/or of the government issuing a deposit guarantee.

Indeed, since the financial crisis developed in 2008, solvency of private banks has been demonstrably different, depending on where, and in which country, it operates and how it is operated.

Finally, we will address the question of countries which have given up on adopting the euro, being that the macroeconomic costs proved too high. This issue thus adds one more dimension to the discussion of what an optimal currency area means in practice.

The core of this chapter will seek to explain how we should understand the macroeconomic consequences of the common European currency. We will investigate why the function of the euro deviates between countries, making the cost and benefits of a common currency fluctuate and become dependent on events. We will also explore the political implications of adopting a common currency, which will prove to be equally important to our study.

A Brief Definition

An 'optimal' currency area may be conceived as a group of separate countries, in which all member states profit economically from participation. In practice, the politically significant requirement is that all countries benefit in a narrow economic sense. Many currency unions are thus underpinned by different kinds of mutual support, redistributive devices and financial transfers. Such arrangements have barely been present within the EMU; instead, each member country is expected to manage its own macroeconomic imbalances, although being a member of a currency union weakens, even erases, some of the traditional policy instruments, such as monetary and exchange rate policies. This lack of mutual support mechanisms, together with a loss of sovereignty, makes the EMU quite different from most other currency unions, such as the federally organised state structure of the United States or Germany.

One of the major conclusions of this book is that it is very unlikely that all member states within the Eurozone will gain from the common currency in economic terms. Imbalances in the foreign trade of goods and financial services prevent this from happening; that is, as soon as the balance-of-payments imbalance starts to accumulate beyond a trivial level of surplus and deficit, countries experience different macroeconomic conditions. Surplus countries create new jobs and grow their GDP because their export of goods and services is larger than their imports. By definition, there is bound to be countries within a monetary union with balance-of-payments deficits, which on the other hand lose jobs and become dependent on foreign borrowing. Deficit countries are the losers in macroeconomics terms. Thus, to keep them within the monetary union, some political or economic compensation should be implemented within the institutional framework (see final chapter).

An Overall Macroeconomic Debate

Macroeconomic theory is no easy task. Indeed, for almost a century, macroeconomists have discussed how to undertake a relevant/macroeconomic analysis. This debate usually gains traction in periods of economic crisis; it became fierce in the 1930s, and continued just after the Second World War. The debate was renewed after the crisis of the 1970s with high rates of inflation; but has not, somewhat surprisingly, really started in the wake of the present financial and social crises.

However, two distinct schools of macroeconomic thinking have crystallised in the course of this long-standing debate. These two schools have taken quite different methodological approaches to macroeconomic analysis (Jespersen 2009) in the long and, until now, unsolved debate. However, to understand the present deep crisis of the Eurozone, we should recognise that there is not one single explanation of the causes of the crisis, just as there is not one single and indispensable macroeconomic policy which all countries have to follow.

To put it very briefly, we are dealing with two schools of macroeconomics: (1) *Neoclassical monetarism* and (2) *Keynesian realism*. Although theirs is a long debate, it can be encapsulated in a few, quite distinct analytical differences; these are laid out in more detail in the following appendix.

Neoclassical Monetarism was developed in the post-War period in opposition to the so-called bastard Keynesian macroeconomic framework – a framework that was dominated by short-term demand management models. These models were correctly criticised for not taking monetary factors and inflation into consideration (see Patinkin 1958; Friedman 1969; Lucas and Sargent 1979).

Neoclassical macroeconomists have always taken microeconomics as their point of analytical departure. They hence present an argument for the single-market model where, sooner or later, demand and supply come to be equalised by price (and wage) flexibility; see, for instance, Mankiw's textbook on *Macroeconomics* (9th ed., 2016). In addition, the assumption is that, when organised according to market economic principles with perfect competition, the entire macroeconomic system will be self-adjusting, in that it creates a general equilibrium for all of the market within a reasonable time span (usually 5–10 years). Hence, if the market system is left to function on its own, without political interventions, it will generate an outcome of full employment, where households and firms have all optimised their utilisation of resources. From an individual point of view, within this general equilibrium model, it is only a lack of price (and wage) flexibility or political intervention that can obstruct the market system to settle in this optimal solution.

It is then clear what policy is required to ensure that this general equilibrium model delivers the best outcome: make each market as flexible as possible, minimise and balance the public sector's budget and control the money supply in order to prevent inflation. Within this model, we can therefore conclude that money is neutral with respect to real economic development, while the only lasting impact is upon price inflation.

Keynes(ian) Realism had to be rediscovered after the setbacks presented by the misguided macroeconomic modelling of the 1960s, when inflation and price-/wage-dynamics were disregarded. In going back to Keynes's *General Theory*, it was argued that the macroeconomic consequences of *uncertainty* – understood as the lack of information about the future and of the working of the macroeconomic system – had hitherto been overlooked and therefore undervalued. However, by looking at the real numbers in the economies of the Eurozone countries, it becomes obvious that the macroeconomic system at the national level was anything but a perfect and self-adjusting market system. Unemployment went up and stayed high in many countries, while inflation was bumpy, financial markets increasingly unstable, and in no respect could one say that the balance-of-payments imbalances were ironed out between the European countries.

In taking such a *realistic* view, macroeconomists should admit that it is no simple task to model the outcome of the macroeconomic system. Even in the short run of 1–3 years ahead, uncertainty plays quite an important and challenging role at the micro as well as the macro level. The impact of this inherent uncertainty has been further amplified by the increased amount of financial deregulation within European economies in combination with governments being prevented from managing demand and having to roll back welfare states, even in periods with rising unemployment.

Instead, according to realist theory, uncertainty can be reduced – though never in any sense completely removed – by setting up robust social and financial institutions. The theoretical point to be developed here is that the market mechanism adds flexibility to the microeconomic system. However, individuals do not base their actions on the knowledge of how the entire macro system works. Hence, the sum of individual decisions (and, for the same reason, expectations) may lead the macro system in any direction. A guiding hand and guiding principles are therefore needed to ensure a stable economy. These are necessarily partly national because countries are impacted to a different degree, for example, due to them having different automatic budget stabilisers. The impact that the individual decisions have on the macro system is also partly mutually experienced by the other countries in the Eurozone because the balance-of-payments deficits cannot be reduced unless surplus countries cooperate.

Within this *realistic* theoretical framework, the decision of a country to abandon its national currency has important implications, being that it decouples the link between the real sector (employment and output) and monetary and exchange rate policies. This delinking cannot at the macro level be compensated for by an increased flexibility of the market mechanism (i.e., labour market reforms) and the financial sectors. It could easily cause further instability. So, without a coordinated federal political structure within the EMU, this lack of national monetary and exchange rate policies could easily make fiscal policy to be overloaded and end up in a public sector debt crisis.

The theoretical debate between *Neoclassical Monetarism* and *Keynes (ian) Realism* has been an important fixture within the macroeconomic academic establishment since the 1930s. When economic crisis is the dominant issue, realism seems to have the upper hand. In more tranquil periods or when market ideology is dominant (for instance, neoliberalism after 1990), the neoclassical paradigm tends to become the mainstream economic argument. Nonetheless, it was John Maynard Keynes who designed the international monetary system after the Second World War, with fixed but adjustable exchange rates and – if Keynes had been the only designer – a symmetric system of adjustment to the balance of payments would have been established.

The realist approach was challenged back in the 1960s by, amongst others, Milton Friedman and Don Patinkin in monetarist/neoclassical attempts to stage what was called a counter-revolution. However, after the breakdown of simple Keynesian macro models during the crises of the 1970s, the neoclassical/monetarist paradigm became mainstream macroeconomics. Here, macro models had to be rooted in rational individual behaviour and microeconomic market analysis with market clearing. This developed into the now dominant general equilibrium model (see, for instance, Lucas 1987).

Evaluation of an 'Optimal Currency Area'

After the breakdown of the international gold standard in the 1930s, the establishment of the Bretton Woods agreement in 1944 set rather strict rules for international money transactions. However, hardly any debate took place regarding whether or not a common/shared currency between two or more independent/sovereign nations was a good idea.

The Canadian economist Robert Mundell made the first theoretical contribution to this question in writing a paper called *A Theory of Optimal Currency Areas* (1961). His project was to establish a scheme of analysis for making a judgement and to determine whether, economically, it would be a good idea for Canada to adopt the American dollar in order to facilitate a rather large cross-border trade, travel expenditure and even, at that time, financial transactions. He made his analysis within a so-called neoclassical-synthesis model, taking inspiration from the so-called Mundell–Fleming model as a forerunner to the neoclassical monetarist model.

In this paper, Mundell differentiates between the lasting microeconomic benefits derived from lower transaction costs related to cross-border trade and, in giving up monetary and exchange rate policies, the temporary loss of policies aiming for macroeconomic stability. In this Canadian case, the U.S. dollar exchange rate would be dominant; thus, if capital controls between the United States and Canada were then lifted, the Canadian central bank would lose control of domestic money supply and the short-term interest rate.

Hence, within this monetarist framework, benefits were related to the size of cross-border transactions. Costs depended on the difference of the business cycle in Canada compared to that in the United States. The argument is that the larger the share of the Canadian GDP that is exported to the United States, the closer the convergence between business cycles of the two countries and the less Canada will need to use her exchange rate and monetary policies for short-run demand management.

Mundell referred to the case of an 'optimal currency area' where benefit exceeds cost; that is, where each participating country would gain by giving up its own currency. However, this constitutes a rather simplistic analysis if the equilibrium framework alone is used. Here, costs are only related to the loss of output during a rather short adjustment period until full employment is regained following any macroeconomic disturbance. The more trust the neoclassical monetarists placed in the equilibrating forces of the market system, the shorter the expected adjustment period, and hence, the loss of output, would be. Furthermore, the more business cycles of the participating countries are synchronised, the more effective a common monetary and exchange rate policy will be in contributing to this equilibrating process. Indeed, monetarists are often somewhat sceptical with respect to the ability of national politicians to undertake longer-running stabilising policies.

On the other hand, Mundell's analysis also demonstrated that in the case of a large number of countries, it was less likely that their business cycles could be synchronised, resulting in higher costs for giving up national policy instruments. The greater the difference between national markets and/or the more the markets had a sluggish nature, especially as regards the labour markets, the larger the adjustment required for the loss of output would be. This also holds within an equilibrium model.

The cost and benefit of joining a monetary union is then quite simple in the monetarist framework. It is usually demonstrated within a diagram, where the degree of economic integration is measured along the x-axis and macroeconomic cost, which are considered as temporary and microeconomic benefits, which are lasting, are measured along the y-axis (see Fig. 2.1).

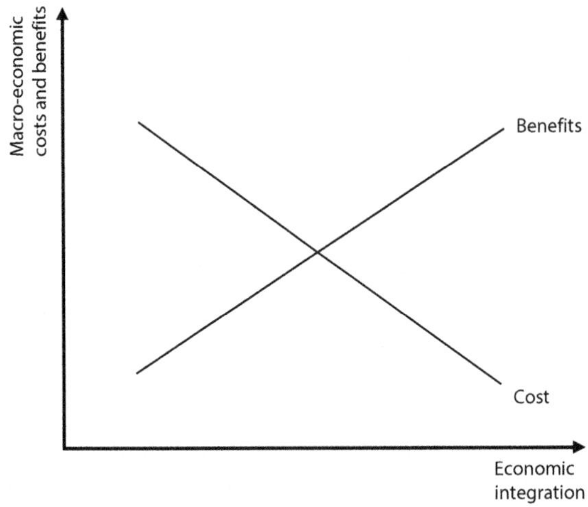

Fig. 2.1 Monetarist presentation of short-term cost and persistent benefit of joining a monetary union

The alternative is to undertake a realist view, but here the analysis becomes much more complicated for a number of reasons. Although the microeconomic gains have been clearly recognised, uncertainty plays a much more significant role in regard to future developments. If, for instance, the decision makers had known that there was a risk of financial markets collapsing, how would they have judged the consequences of running a balance-of-payments deficit and the loss of a nationally determined rate of interest and exchange rate? This means that macroeconomic cost could also easily be persistent and even growing through time. A full analysis would also have to integrate the response of the other member states, especially with regard to balance-of-payments considerations.

Furthermore, looking more broadly at the Eurozone, when the international financial markets collapsed, countries with a rather large foreign debt/export ratio and a substantial balance-of-payments deficit (current foreign borrowing requirement) were hit hard. The macroeconomic costs of foreign debt were then considerable, invalidating the argument that the balance of payments would cease to be a macroeconomic constraint. The financial market obviously under-estimated the debtor risk in relation to financing the balance of payments' deficit and the adjustment costs. This risk/uncertainty then increased in proportion with the size of foreign trade.

Hence, the empirical evidence is ambiguous in regard to the hypothesis of a monetary union promoting more trans-border trade. Glick and Rose (2015) also admit that, with regard to the trade-promoting effects, their previous, rather optimistic conclusion might be misleading.[1]

Hence, when economic integration is increased, the overall macroeconomic cost might not fall because the country integrated has become more dependent on international competitiveness.

A realist analysis would therefore add this increased uncertainty and macroeconomic cost of foreign debt. Furthermore, the self-adjustment mechanism of the macroeconomic system might either be too weak or may not exist at all, leaving a Euro member state in a position of permanently under-utilised output capacity and under-employment. In such cases, the cost of giving up an exchange rate policy may be substantial, leaving the question of whether an 'optimal currency area' without any transfer mechanism to compensate losers could ever be anything like an 'Optimal Currency Area'.

Appendix: Two Schools of Euro-Macroeconomics

Introduction

We cannot fully engage in a macroeconomic discussion about a monetary union within the EU (EMU) without being aware that two very divergent analytical frameworks are in use:

1. *A neoclassical framework* we could call euro-monetarism, developed by Robert Mundell and supported by a number of scholars, using a general equilibrium model as their analytical starting point.
2. *A realist framework,* taking its inspiration from post-Keynesian and institutional theories, and supported by a number of realists taking their departure from empirical evidence.

Euro-monetarism

Euro-monetarism takes as its point of departure the very simple demand and supply diagram well known to neoclassical microeconomics. This diagram is then used to explain the equilibrium in a number of macro-markets:

1. Labour markets
2. GDP markets
3. Capital markets
4. Foreign exchange markets

The equilibrating variable is the 'macro price' for each market, the money wage rate, the GDP deflator, the interest rate and the exchange rate.

In a general equilibrium macroeconomic model, all the assumptions of the conventional neoclassical 'perfect' market model are represented:

1. Individual optimisation
2. Perfect foresight, that is, rational expectations
3. Many competitors and perfect competition
4. Flexible price/wage adjustments (equilibrating each market)

In addition, this is important:

5. A general equilibrium solution to the entire model is taken for granted. If all market prices are fully flexible, then the model will – by itself – generate a general equilibrium, which, according to the microeconomic foundations and related assumptions is a so-called Pareto Optimal solution.

According to this general equilibrium model, countries will always subscribe to the idea of an 'optimal currency area'. Here, the permanent benefits of the common currency providing lower transactions costs will always outweigh the costs of short-term macroeconomic mal-adjustment; that is, as long as we hold the assumption that the macroeconomic system is self-adjusting. Any macroeconomic deviation from the general equilibrium is then assumed to be caused either by a lack of price-/wage-flexibility or by a policy encroachment.

We have presented a prime example of how euro-monetarists do not connect their arguments to reality. Even a relatively open-minded euro-monetarist like Paul De Grauwe writes, in a fairly recent edition of his textbook, that 'The recent Eurozone crisis lends some credence to the view that the present Eurozone is not an optimal currency area' (p. 78).

Euro-realism

Realist macroeconomics asks the question: What can we know from real-world observations in regard to macroeconomic imbalances? Here it becomes obvious that unemployment, a budget deficit and imbalances of payments are all integral to the understanding of the economic developments in the EMU countries. Moreover, serious macroeconomic imbalances are not only a post-crisis situation. They have been a part of reality ever since the EMU was established. It is important also to emphasise that the imbalances have grown within the EMU as a whole and also between the participating countries during the 17 years of EMU.

In general, reality simply does not support the neoclassical assumption of a self-adjusting macroeconomic system. In fact, the empirical data indicate that the exact opposite is the case:

1. Unemployment is close to its highest ever for the entire EMU period.
2. The variance of unemployment amongst the EU countries has never been higher.
3. Balance-of-payments imbalances and foreign debt have grown between member countries.
4. Differences in real effective exchange rates have exceeded 30 percentage points compared to 1999.
5. Real economic growth rates are deviating more and more.
6. Long-term interest rates are more diverse than ever.

Moreover, a neoclassical general equilibrium model is of little use in explaining these macroeconomic developments. One should instead set up an analytical framework where persistent imbalances can be explained and, to that end, a post-Keynesian analytical model is useful. Here, effective demand is the driving force (see Jespersen 2012). The textbook 'Introduction to Macroeconomics' (Jespersen 2013/2007, English version) provides a fundamental/comprehensive/basic starting point for such an analytical endeavour.

Effective demand could be thought of as the analytical pivot insofar as it is defined as the output of goods and services on the part of the private sector, given a set of uncertain expectations: aggregate domestic and foreign demand, profitability, availability of credit, finance, technology and qualified labour. In the original Keynes model, entrepreneurs will hire people after having decided on how much to produce in the coming period. Hence, where 80 percent of workers constitute unskilled labour, the employment function has rather a simple relationship in this model. In contrast, the 'employment function' is much more complicated for a modern society with more diversified labour and a higher degree of foreign competition. In the end, employment is determined by effective demand.

Hence, together with profitability, entrepreneurs' expectations of future sales constitute the crucial variables for consideration. However, expectations about the future cannot, in reality, be assumed with any degree of certainty (i.e., the neoclassical assumption). One would take quite the contrary to be the case, being that expectations of the entrepreneurs are by nature uncertain; that is, they are related to the unknowable future. Hence, the most challenging question to pose is how entrepreneurs form expectations in an environment constituted by uncertain information about the future and, in particular, the impact of a common currency.

Note

1. 'In our European Economic Review (2002) paper, we used pre-1998 data on countries participating in and leaving currency unions to estimate the effect of currency unions on trade using (then-) conventional gravity models. In this paper, we use a variety of empirical gravity models to estimate the currency union effect on trade and exports, using recent data which includes the European Economic and Monetary Union (EMU). We have three findings. First, our assumption of symmetry between the effects of entering and leaving a currency union seems reasonable in the data but is uninteresting. Second, EMU typically has a smaller trade effect than other currency unions, often estimated to be negligible or negative. Third and most importantly, estimates of the currency union effect on trade are sensitive to the exact econometric methodology; we find no substantive reliable and robust effect of currency union on trade'. From the summary of the Glick and Rose (2015) paper.

CHAPTER 3

Why Was the EMU Established? Different Perspectives

Abstract The European Monetary Union suggested in the late 1980s was considered by the euro-monetarist as a political project to promote further economic integration and to prevent Germany from becoming the dominant European power after re-unification.

The institutions surrounding the European Monetary Union were designed according to the Euro-monetarists' theory of how to create an Optimal Currency Area (OCA) recommended by the Delors Commission (Report on economic and monetary union in the European community, Office for Official Publications of the EC, Luxemburg, 1989). Hence, politics overruled any realist objection by defining loose convergence criteria making too many countries eligible for the common currency and by disregarding balance-of-payments imbalances. Furthermore, the unilateral focus on the public sector deficit without viewing private sector imbalances underestimated the structural differences between the potential member states.

Had a Euro-realist analytical framework been employed, a number of these macroeconomic imbalances would have been addressed at an earlier stage with less devastating consequences.

Keywords Convergence criteria without convergence · Stability pact without stability · Lack of realism · One size does not fit all Euro countries · Macroeconomics imbalances

J. Jespersen, *The Euro*, DOI 10.1007/978-3-319-46388-9_3

Introduction

In the 1960s, certain European voices promoted the belief that a single currency would support economic and political integration in Europe (including the Werner Report, 1972). 'One Market, One Money' was often whispered in the corridors of Brussels; it appeared as something almost self-evident and was referred to much as, inter alia, one would mention a European football team or a European community anthem. Indeed, European policy ambition was to provide a counterweight to ever-prevailing national sentiment, and the Brussels elite set out to redirect these national sentiments towards Europe, particularly since, in the 1960s and 1970s, the shadow of Charles de Gaulle's 'empty chair' policy still had an influence on the integrationist reflections of high-ranking politicians.

However, the 'One Market, One Money' rhetoric was not immediately supported by the majority of national politicians. Ambitious European policy proposals for a single currency ran into a deadlock each time the proposals were put forward by the EU Commission. The governments of member states were doubtful about how realistic the proposal was in both economic and political terms. Just like today, differences between the countries' economic structures and political aspirations were significant, and stronger arguments had to be developed before member states would renounce their sovereignty of printing money and agree to a fixed exchange rate.

Nonetheless, following the breakdown of the Bretton Woods system in 1973, a kind of monetary cooperation was established within the European Economic Community (EEC) based on a French–German initiative in 1979. Moreover, the UK remained on a 'waiting list' for entering the monetary union until the late 1980s. However, the working of the European Monetary System (EMS) was not considered a success. Currency crises occurred frequently through the 1980s, partly because of the size of the fluctuation band, which was maintained at a very narrow ±2 ¼ per cent. Hence, the participating countries quickly realised that those countries with a balance-of-payments surplus became more and more dominant, even causing some of the deficit countries to drop out.

During the 1980s, Germany and the Netherlands accumulated huge trade surpluses, which caused growing foreign debt in the other EMS countries and increased difficulties in getting loans on the international finance market. These economic and financial imbalances have created a division of power within the EMS (and the EEC), insofar as surplus countries have been able to dictate interest rate policy throughout the EMS zone. Deficit countries have had to borrow overseas, or leave the EMS and let the exchange rate be determined by market forces.

The United Kingdom experienced such a sequence during its short life as an EMS member country. She joined the fixed exchange rate mechanism in 1989, but was then forced to leave following heavy and costly speculation against the pound in September 1992. Other countries such as Italy (and France) stepped in and out of the Exchange Rate Mechanism (ERM), dependent on how divergent they were economically and politically with the increasingly dominating German D-mark and Bundesbank. Smaller countries such as Denmark and Belgium then made a number of smaller devaluations, which annoyed the German monetary representatives. Instead, Germany recommended that member countries with a weak balance of payments should aim for more labour market discipline and reduced money wage inflation to overcome macroeconomic imbalances.

Hence, the working of the EMS was an illustration of how difficult it is to run a fixed exchange rate system among rather different nation stats. As long as there was no obligation for the surplus countries to act, the adjustment pressure was solely at the shoulders of the deficit countries. Why should surplus countries reduce its strong competitive position creating jobs and foreign wealth? The only risk at that time, which the Germans had to consider, was the threat of other member countries to leave – especially France. So, Germany agreed hesitantly to revaluate the D-mark when larger exchange rate realignments were needed during the 1980s and early 1990. The problem with these exchange rates adjustments that they were always too late and too little, which made it a piece of cake for speculators to gain a lot. So, tensions built up. The Euro-monetarists argued that the only way to get rid of these continuous waves of speculation would be to establish one and only one currency in the EU. But they did not explain where the tensions from differences in competitiveness and balance-of-payments imbalances would go?

However, tensions continued to build up within the EMS. A number of countries were leaving the fixed exchange rate system, most notably UK and Italy, as well as the Nordic countries except Denmark that left in the year 1992/93 and the exchange system stood on the brink of collapse.

This near breakdown occurred in the background of the new EU Treaty (the Maastricht Treaty) when the proposed common European currency was in the process of being ratified by the national parliaments of the member countries. Finally, this delicate situation was solved in a very pragmatic way by enlarging the accepted band of exchange rate fluctuations from ±2.25 percent to ±15 percent. The EMS hence survived in name alone with fundamental changes to its character. The system moved from a rigid fixed rate system to a very flexible system with possible fluctuations of 30 per cent (two times 15 per cent). This would be very costly and, in practice, unlikely to force participating countries to change the parity through pure speculation.

Nonetheless, governments gained the time necessary either to change domestic policies or to make an orderly devaluation. In consequence, the EMS did calm down for the rest of the 1990s, while the Treaty of Maastricht was approved in France via a referendum, albeit with a very narrow margin, and then by the national parliament.

A 'Common' European Currency Became a Political Project Supported by the Euro-monetarists

Unfortunately, when the Delors Commission was established in 1988 (Jacques Delors was at that time chairman of the EU Commission), there was no practical learning process available for managing a fixed exchange rate system and organising European monetary affairs within an integrating European economy to the benefit of all EU member countries. The appropriate measures to ensure this were therefore not taken and, with the process of establishing a 'single European market for goods' being set to finish in 1992, the project of creating a common European currency was re-launched. Aiming for an 'ever closing Union', the EU Commission saw the common currency as a useful vehicle for further integration. The EU Commission needed approval from the national central bank governors and independent economic experts in order to convince the heads of states and governments to agree to create a common currency. Hence, the so-called Delors Commission was established with the central bank governors of twelve member countries as participants and three 'independent' economic experts from the school of euro-monetarism. The Commission's task was to propose a roadmap for changing the European Monetary System (EMS) to better support the market for goods, capital and labour and hereby promote the aim of 'ever closer union', listed in the preamble to the EU Treaty.

The proposal to establish an economic monetary union (EMU) within the EEC (as it was still called) was thus presented in the spring of 1989 based on the Delors Commission's work. However, it was given further momentum by the fall of the Berlin Wall in autumn 1989 and the re-unification of Germany that was achieved the year after.

After re-unification, Germany would be the EEC's most populous member state and its largest economy. This shift in economic and political strength would inevitably leave its mark on the future of the Community's cooperation. Not least France feared the rise of German dominance. This was not perceived as an immediate threat, as Germany had gotten her hands more than full with integrating the two very different German economies – but rather it was feared to happen in the longer term.

In fact, re-unification had weakened German dominance in the short term and France saw a unique opportunity to strengthen European cooperation at the expense of Germany. This proved an opportunity that the Commission was quick to support, if not to take full advantage of. Evidently, the Commission was aware that the EU was nothing like an OCA, but a clear window of opportunity had been presented. The eventual macroeconomic imbalances that would follow was thus to be handled like all the other previous setbacks, which had characterised the working of the EU, and would be overcome by new initiatives. This is the so-called neo-functionalistic approach to European dynamic integration: to solve a crisis by proposing greater European integration.

The German officials, and especially the governor of the Bundesbank, Carl Otto Pöhl, had, as mentioned in the previous chapter, some reservations with regard to the numbers and the differences in economic structures of the potential member that an OCA could comprise. But the French president in collaboration with the European Commission brushed these reservations aside. They shared an interest in reducing German domination together with the aim of instating a future European currency to be used by nearly 500 million inhabitants and backed by the world's largest GDP. This neo-functionalistic attitude revealed that the process of establishing a single European currency was predominantly a politically motivated one. From the very beginning, Great Britain and Denmark asked to be exempted from the paragraphs of the Maastricht Treaty related to the common currency. This exclusion should have been read as a warning signal that Europe was still not ready for monetary unification. The expectations of both France and the Euro-monetarists as regards the establishment of a common currency were quite different from what the actual outcome came to be. At that time, the French had not understood from the previous experiences with the EMS that it was not the Germany's currency per se that was responsible for the dominance of the West German economy in the 1970s and 1980s. It was rather the strong competitive position of Germany's industry, which did not promise to weaken any time soon. This failed analysis was supported by the Euro-monetarists, who did not recognise a permanent balance-of-payments surplus to be an inherent problem for a monetary union. Instead, they argued that fully integrated financial capital markets would iron out any such imbalance.

France and the Euro-monetarists believed that if monetary policy within the future European Central Bank (ECB) could be decided by a majority vote, then France would regain a great deal of the lost influence upon the interest and exchange rate policy of the EU. In fact, it was agreed that, in the future, monetary policy would be determined by the ECB's board of directors, represented by one director from each participating country. This way, the core of economic 'hard-liner' member states would not dominate decision making (besides Germany, these countries also counted the Netherlands, Austria and Finland).

As a consequence, contrary to German wishes, the French EMU proposal adopted by the European Council contained a number of relatively 'soft' admission criteria for the EU member states to join the EMU. Here, political considerations were once again at stake, rather than economic insights when the soft criteria for being accepted as a Euro member were formulated. The question of which countries would be judged to have a sufficiently uniform economic structure to become part of the EMU was not on the political agenda; instead, a large number of participating countries were considered to successfully fulfil the primary criteria for membership (in regard to the lack of debate here, see Hoffmeyer 2005)

The French position was summarised by President François Mitterrand in the following phrase: 'Rather a European Germany than a German Europe'. However, his analysis proved to be wrong.

Convergence Criteria without Convergence

A major role in the Euro's early history was hence played by admission requirements, or convergence criteria. The Maastricht Treaty listed four relatively lenient requirements together with the public sector deficit not exceeding 3 of GDP to be fulfilled in order for states to become members of the EMU. However, as criteria written into the EU Treaty, they showed to be impossible to change at a later stage. Furthermore, the Treaty required that EU countries that did conform to the convergence criteria had to adopt the common currency.

Hence, an unfortunate situation arose in which interests of France and the EU Commission, who both wanted as large a membership as possible, coincided with the interests of the weaker EU economies, for whom membership of the 'European currency' was considered a 'seal of approval'. For the weaker countries, membership of the EMU became a matter of national prestige. From their perspective, only successful economies would be admitted, while they perceived failure to be admitted as demotion to second-class status in the EU. Unsurprisingly, the question of membership thus became a politically sensitive issue. In this game of political prestige, the theoretical question of a country becoming a part of a European OCA slid into the background, with the result that all the 'old' EU countries that wanted to join the EMU duly became members.

The main criticism of the convergence criteria was that it only required fulfilment in a single year, entailing that any government so desiring could make the figures add up without much difficulty. Even the German finance minister, Theo Weigel, suggested that, when the German budget deficit surpassed the 3 per cent of GDP, the Bundesbank could sell off parts of its gold reserves. Such a sale would be registered as a resource for the German state, resulting in a reduction of the German budget deficit.

Hence, considerable creativity was demonstrated by many countries to comply with these rather soft and unsatisfying criteria, which furthermore only had to be fulfilled in a single year (except for membership of EMS). The example of Germany illustrates the absurdity of the definition of the budget requirement; the selling off of public property was considered to be on equal terms with raising taxes. The inadequate and arbitrary definition of how the public sector budget deficit should be calculated has continued to haunt the Euro member states since the very start of the project.

However, the tendency for states to fulfil the convergence criteria in only a single year was not the only criticism levied by the Euro-realists. Let us briefly review the four principal criticisms one by one.

1. **Price stability**: The rate of inflation of consumer goods in the member states should not exceed the inflation rate in the three member countries that have proved best at keeping prices stable by more than 1.5 points.

The objection here is that competition within the EU internal market itself ensures that the tradable part of consumer goods will at least resemble each other. However, in relation to the good function of the EMU, this point is trivial compared, for instance, to the importance given to the ability of cost levels to develop in parallel in order to secure profitability. To put it another way: just because a hand blender costs the same all across the Eurozone does not mean that the cost inflation of every country is convergent.

2. **Stable currency**: Each member state must respect the normal limits of fluctuations in the exchange rate (±15 percent) within the European Exchange Rate Mechanism (ERM) for at least 2 years.

   As mentioned earlier, ± 15 percent comes close to a floating exchange rate. However, this is hardly a test, and a far better criterion would have been to focus on the balance of payments; for instance, with no deficit or surplus exceeding 3 percent of GDP and foreign debt remaining smaller than 40 percent of GDP.

3. **Stable long rate of interest**: Within the test year, member states may not, on average, have had a long-term interest rate deviating by more than 2 percentage points compared to the three best-performing member countries.

   This was mainly a test of the expectations of the financial markets. If membership were the dominant expectation, then the exchange rate risk would disappear. At that time, government bonds (without exchange rate risk) were rated AAA; hence, if the other criteria were met, then speculators would consider any government bond to be almost as safe as a German one. However, this assumption was wrong, although it was not proved as such until after 2008. Until then, speculation on the European capital markets mirrored conventional wisdom.

4. **Sustainable public finances**: The annual public deficit should not exceed 3 per cent of GDP. Likewise, the public debt should not exceed 60 per cent of GDP.

   A standard number of 3 percent was arbitrarily chosen, although no one could explain where this had come from. Some critique focused on the inadequate procedure of lumping all expenditure and revenue together, as though they were on the same footing. For example, unemployment benefits, the selling of gold and the construction of new infrastructures were all taken to add up to just

> a single figure, as if old age pension, education and new railways were to be handled as the exact same product when reductions of expenditures were required. A concrete example of this is the Greek government currently being required to sell off some of its islands to make them the private reserve for the rich/private property of wealthy private owners.

The focus on public sector balance is an outcome of the euro-monetarist way of thinking, where the private sector is taken as self-adjusting via the market mechanism and competition. Hence, any public sector imbalance will obstruct the processes of private sector adjustment. A realist economist would instead examine empirically where the cause of macroeconomic imbalance should be found. The answer, as we shall see, could equally well be that the balance of payments, over-saving in the private sector or lack of effective demand in the labour market spills over into the public sector via automatic budget stabilisers.

As we shall see, the only worry seriously expressed by the Euro-monetarists (and the German Bundesbank) was the risk of politicians not keeping the public sector budget below 3 per cent of GDP. By the end of the 1990s, the requirement was therefore the introduction of the so-called Stability and Growth Pact to be part of the EU Treaty (Amsterdam Treaty). This will be explored in the next section.

Despite the critique from Euro-realists and the prolonged financial crisis, which has vindicated that the Eurozone, in its present form, does not come close being to an OCA, the convergence criteria have not been changed. Although it is obvious that the new member states are, in many respects, non-convergent, Brussels has continued to welcome them into the Eurozone. On the other hand, countries such as Sweden, Poland and the Czech Republic without a formal euro-opt out clause have deliberately avoided being members of the EMU by not fulfilling all five convergence criteria. They have simply not applied for membership of the European fixed exchange rate system, ERM (formerly called EMS) and just led their currencies float against the euro. These countries did so for at least two principal reasons. First, the political leaders realised that the popular resistance to the Euro was so strong that it could jeopardise the countries' membership of the EU. Second, they considered the common currency to be just a stepping stone to further political integration. Accordingly, it was not the ruling political class that held these reservations, but rather the citizens. In Sweden and Denmark, a referendum was held in which the government strongly recommended an acceptance of the Euro, but a majority of the people voted against it.[1]

The More Members of the Monetary Union, the Weaker It Becomes

The single European currency became a reality in 1999. Originally, the Eurozone counted eleven and quite soon twelve (Greece was accepted in 2002) of the fifteen 'old' EU members. In 2004, the EU was enlarged with ten new member states, of which seven – all minor economies – have later become members of the EMU.

In Brussels, the dominant viewpoint is still that the more members of the EMU, the greater its success. Hence, the EU Commission has no plans to redesign the convergence criteria. Decision makers would have stopped enlarging the EMU had they adopted the perspective of Euro-realists in regard to the main content of the theory of an 'OCA'. However, the Brussels elite did not adhere to the economic argument presented by Realists and disregarded the reality that a number of southern and eastern European countries had primarily wanted to become members for political reasons.

To change the convergence criteria would, of course, have opened up the old debate as to whether European integration should take the form of a one-speed or a multi-speed process. Multiple speeds would have entailed a split into first-class members (the core members) with the closest degree of cooperation and a dominant voice in European matters, and members who have different kinds of exemptions from the EU Treaty and are therefore treated as second-class members. More recently, it is precisely this latter differentiation that the UK had objected strongly against.

The southern European countries had a desire to go on to be first class because it would also allow them, as it was argued, to draw on the greater creditworthiness of the stronger EU economies. Hence, the relaxed convergence criteria had helped them to become members of the EMU. Here, one can observe in parentheses that, although the convergence criteria were already accommodating to a majority of the countries, even Germany and France had difficulties in qualifying for membership, which should have caused them to re-examine the feasibility of the entire project. This also came as a surprise to the EMU fathers, the Euro-monetarists, and should have been interpreted as a warning sign. Instead, it contributed to an even more lax attitude towards the convergence criteria and the 60 per cent limit on public debt was disregarded, which saved Italy, Belgium and Greece from not being excluded from the membership of the Eurozone.

It became obvious that the greater the number of countries participating in a monetary union, the smaller the gains for any of the countries, if any gains at all. This asymmetry grew proportionally in accordance to the number of member countries. Those countries that already at the initial stage were highly integrated economically, such as Germany, the Benelux countries and Austria, and a rather similar economic structure could probably be said to be capable of forming an OCA. But, even though the economic arguments are in favour of a common currency, the junior partners have to cope with being dominated politically by. This is the reason why Canada governments have never seriously considered adopting a common currency with the United States, because that would in practice be a US dollar.

But looking at the economic development in France, not to speak of Italy and Spain, before and again after the adaptation of a common currency with Germany shows that the proposition of these countries being able to form an OCA could not and can still not be substantiated. Hereby, a genuine dilemma for these countries has been established. The euro as a means of exchange is quite popular in southern Europe, and the connection between the adaptation of the euro, the German economic dominance and macroeconomic break down is not obvious to the ordinary people (see Pew Research Centre, *Faith in European Project Reviving*, June 2015).

In the Eastern Europe, there has also been a fascination with the Euro, but the unavoidable loss of sovereignty has become an increasing problem for the ruling political class here, entailing that they are hesitant to adopt the common currency and submit to supervision from Brussels. One needs only to glance at what has happened to the living standards and the rising number of poor people in southern Europe, see Chapter 6 to understand why countries with a responsible political leadership want to keep its monetary sovereignty for the time being. This distrust in EU institutions has been further strengthened by the lack of solidarity demonstrated by the attitut forward by the 'Institutions' when deficit countries applied for an EU loan.

In fact, the consequences of overly weak convergence criteria, combined with lax interpretation, plagued the EMU right from the very beginning. Meetings of the European Council were dominated by an agenda fixed on the question, 'What are we to do with the functions of the EMU?', which used up most of the time available without a lasting solution being found.

Stability Pact without Stability

By the mid-1990s, the euro appeared likely to become a reality by the end of the century. The Germans demanded a more permanent stability criterion, when it became clear that the weak convergence criteria did not, by themselves, constitute any guarantee that the countries involved would actually be convergent. Both the governments of Germany and the Bundesbank feared that some of the Social Democratic-led countries would take a more relaxed attitude to public finances under the umbrella of German creditworthiness. The German government predominantly held the Euro-monetarist view favouring the discipline of a highly competitive private market economy with an emphasis on a balanced public sector budget. Accordingly, the German government required that a 'Stability Pact' containing these two elements was accepted by all member countries of the EU and written into the Amsterdam Treaty by 1997.

The goal of the Stability Pact was a permanent reduction of public deficits to a maximum of 3 of GDP supported by an aim of a balanced budget in the medium-term perspective of 2–3 years. To subscribe to the Euro-monetarist position is to consider a public sector deficit as a disruptive element within a market system. Public intervention, if any, should then be to correct market failures without interference in the working of the proper market mechanisms. As an important part of the Euro-monetarist approach, the theory of public choice is applied to policy making. Here it is assumed that politicians like *homo economicus* are promoting initiatives for the sake of self-optimisation and, therefore, are under the suspicion of using public money for re-election purposes instead of favouring pure market solutions. Therefore, Euro-monetarists recommend that strict budget discipline is enforced upon elected politicians via the constitution. For the same reason, the European Central Bank (ECB) is explicitly exempted in the EU Treaty from any official political interference.

Shortly before the Stability Pact was agreed upon by the European Council, a general election was called in France by the then president, Jacques Chirac. The new socialist government required re-negotiation of the Stability Pact. The only visible change was the name, which was changed to the 'Stability and Growth Pact', but with exactly the same content. This approach signalled, first, the dominance of Germany, and second, that the new French government subscribed by and large to the Euro-monetarist way of thinking, one shared by Gerhard Schröder in Germany and Tony Blair in the United Kingdom, both supporting the so-called Third Way in politics, where a liberal welfare state agenda is combined with growing globalisation. The fate of the Stability Pact has its own inherent irony. One of the first countries to break the Stability Pact's 3 per cent rule was Germany closely followed by France in 2003 and 2004, demonstrating that, in reality, EU rules do not always apply to the larger member states. France and Germany argued that their difficulties were a 'special case' and that they were entitled to get exemptions from the 'Stability Pact' with the support of other Euro member states. The latter then saw a window of flexibility, which some of them took advantage of later. The Commission brought a lawsuit to the European Court of Justice claiming that the European Council of Ministers had made a decision not to comply with the Treaty. The EU Commission then had to reconsider two principal propositions: (1) That larger countries hold a special position and may have a greater influence on what is considered as possible within the EU (2) From now on, a more pragmatic attitude with regard to saving the Euro would be given higher priority than the letter of the EU Treaty.

Conclusion: The Inherent Contradictions of the EMU

One of Mundell's main conclusions was that a currency union can only function without suffering major problems if member states are quite similar in terms of both their standard of living (i.e. economic structures) and political preferences (by which Mundell aims to strike a balance between growth, employment and inflation). If member states are too different with economic crises impacting them very differently (asymmetrical shocks), then they quickly come to the realisation that the macroeconomic costs are often very unevenly distributed between the countries.

The reduced number of policy instruments and the increased foreign and domestic debt accumulated in the Euro area would cause difficulties for member countries when seeking to establish better macroeconomic balances represented by less unemployment, smaller balance of payments deficit and reduced public debt ratio.

Within a Euro-monetarist model, the answer to such instances of increased macroeconomic imbalance is an 'internal devaluation', that is, reduced wage costs. In reality, as we shall see, internal cost reduction is not easy to undertake for a number of reasons: (1) Money wages in the private sector are difficult to reduce except for minimum wage earners and other weak social groups who are seldom employed in competitive industries (except for tourism); (2) If the real wage is reduced significantly, then this entails a lack of domestic demand, which, depending on the openness of the country under consideration, can only be partly compensated for by an improved balance of payments; and (3) reduced income in nominal terms means a higher real cost of debt servicing in the private and public sector, causing an increased threat of bankruptcy to households and firms.

There is an obvious difference within the socio-economic priorities of growth and inflation between the north, south and east of Europe. In the early 2000s, the Northern European economies became more and more competitive due to low money wage increases at the expense of low growth. Southern Europe then took advantage of significantly lower interest rates and accepted much higher GDP growth at the expense of the balance of payments. This development was reflected in growing foreign surpluses and deficits dividing Europe between north and south.

The Euro-monetarists had nothing to say to this imbalance, where the private sector in the south became more and more indebted by borrowing in the northern banks, which had accumulated an excess of lending capacity due to balance-of-payments surpluses. Market economists considered this development as an outcome of rational private decisions. They limited their focus to public sector finances, which were doing reasonably well in the relatively fast-growing south – until it came to a sudden stop when the financial crisis stroke and created distrust and lack of lending capacity between banks and between countries.

Fuelled by Euro-monetarist arguments related to the possibility of creating an OCA within Europe, the fathers of the common European currency were very optimistic. Their optimism made them suggest rather weak convergence criteria and a Stability Pact only related to a balanced public sector budget. Had they investigated the very unrealistic assumptions behind the Euro-optimistic view more closely, they might have been more cautious. However, within a theoretical model, one can only derive an outcome which corresponds to the assumptions one has made. If one assumes that the Eurozone will converge to full employment within a limited number of years, then the model will support this optimistic view.

Hence, there has been no shortage of Euro-optimistic analyses demonstrating that even if the Euro countries may not initially constitute an OCA, increased mutual trade would ensure that the benefits outlined by the Euro-monetarists would exceed costs within a few years (See, for instance Rose 2000; De Grauwe 1999). On the other hand, US monetarists such as Friedman were much less optimistic. They doubted, within the same model, that wage flexibility would be able to secure balance-of-payments adjustments within a reasonable time horizon.

However, few or no one in and around Brussels dared to mention, or even came to think that the common currency was premature. Such a thought would have been highly politically contentious, going against the predominant 'Federal-European' ideal. The common currency was, in Brussels, seen as the vehicle to put Europe at the world map and an indispensable sign of the coming European unity. So, the argument that 'the Euro was a problem' was considered in Brussels as a no-go. Such a debate could be the start of ordinary people questioning the rationality behind the Euro, and where would that lead? It is an irony that this suppression of the real problems of the Eurozone were not addressed and therefore grew, so that they ran out of control and eventually became the beginning of the end of the movement towards an 'ever closer Union'. Had these objections been addressed while imbalances were much smaller, and had surplus countries understood that they had to make a positive contribution to the working of the monetary system and to express some solidarity with deficit member state, then the euro might not have failed. But to maintain that, it was primarily the budget deficits and the inflexibility of labour market, which caused the difficulties without addressing the balance-of-payments imbalances, was not helpful. This is the content of the coming chapters.

Note

1. To be honest I am still puzzled why the social democratic government in Sweden and Denmark were so eager to give up the national monetary sovereignty.

CHAPTER 4

Balance-of-Payments *Im*balances have Become the 'Achilles Heel' of the EMU

Abstract A balance-of-payments deficit has to be financed abroad either by the private or by the public sector. This is independent of what currency is in use. If a deficit country is excluded from foreign capital markets, it goes bankrupt. A number of Eurozone countries were harshly reminded of this when the European capital markets froze in 2009/2010.

Euro-monetarist equilibrium theory often confuses foreign deficit with public deficit. Within a monetary union, deficit countries are at the mercy of the surplus countries, because they have renounced their monetary and exchange rate sovereignty. They have made themselves dependent on the borrowing conditions set by the creditors, in case of Germany, ECB and IMF all guided by monetarist thinking and policies.

Narrow limits on balance-of-payments deficit and surplus would make the EMU countries less divergent.

Keywords Balance-of-payments deficit · Creditor countries dictate borrowing conditions · Foreign deficit is different from public deficit · Loss of monetary sovereignty

Introduction

Within a monetary union in which sovereign countries share a common currency, the balance of payments constitutes a mutually interrelated macroeconomic system. This means that the surplus in the current account of one of the member states is a deficit in the account of one or

J. Jespersen, *The Euro*, DOI 10.1007/978-3-319-46388-9_4

more of the other members. The overall current account of the monetary union is due to the externally floating euro exchange rate close to being balanced. But, the imbalances between member economies are, broadly speaking, an unavoidable consequence, when member countries have a different development in growth, production cost or asymmetric shocks. Germany, the largest economy of the Eurozone, managed to improve its competitive position vis-à-vis the other Euro-members, building up an increasing current account surplus and accumulating huge foreign wealth. But this made the deficit countries dependent on borrowing in Germany, eventually causing the cross-border financial relationship to come to a sudden stop when the financial crisis emerged and private banks' solvency was challenged, particularly in the southern European countries.

It has been realised too late that a monetary union cannot work properly if one or more countries are allowed to run persistent and structural surpluses in their current account. In doing so, they drain the deficit countries of liquidity without there being any commitment to recycle the financial surplus. Deficit countries are consequently forced to restrain their imports through austerity policies, which hamper economic growth.

The asymmetry of the working of the EMU has not yet fully been recognised by Euro-monetarists. They have mainly focused on the public sector deficits as a challenge to the proper functioning of the EMU. Euro-realists have then questioned this focus from an empirical perspective.

Balance of Payment *Im*balances are Destabilising the Eurozone

Within a monetary union, trade makes participating countries dependent on each other in both economic and political terms. When a good is bought abroad, then purchasing power is taken out of domestic circulation. If a country is buying more abroad (importing) than it is selling (exporting), then there will be a drain of purchasing power and a need to borrow abroad.

It is a well-known macroeconomic phenomenon that a negative trade balance means a loss of production and jobs to the benefit of the trading partners. A positive trade balance has hence been given high priority by policy makers, ever since the seventeenth century when the mercantilists set the political economic agenda. In modern terms, a surplus at the balance-of-payments current account means that there is significantly more leeway in domestic policy due to the additional liquidity available.

However, and here we come to the core essence of the argument of this book, no modern economy can maintain a surplus on the current account of the balance of payments. Surpluses and deficits have to add up to zero – a simple book-keeping principle that any respectable macroeconomic theory has to reflect.

This simple book-keeping principle applies independently of whether the countries under consideration use, as means of payments, the same currency or different currencies. If a country spends more on imports than it earns on export, then there is a lack of income – that is, a negative saving position – which can only be rectified by either selling assets abroad (running down foreign exchange reserves) or, more commonly, by borrowing abroad. However, in many cases, borrowing abroad is not without political conditions; for governments, in particular, it is quite different to borrow abroad compared with obtaining domestic credit. It makes an important difference for a government to keep its monetary sovereignty and the right to printing money.

Although it is correct that the unit of account becomes the same, when a common currency is introduced, it does not make borrowing abroad more easy. There is still a specific credit risk related to the country under consideration, which foreign banks have to take into account. So, borrowing abroad becomes increasingly difficult when foreign debt accumulates, whether the currency at home and abroad is the same.

Therefore, we should recognise that the size of the foreign debt plays an even more significant role within a monetary union, particularly when there are no formal rules between the participating countries with regard to clearing mechanisms between surplus and deficit member states. Within a federal state – Germany, for instance – rather strong legal transfer mechanisms are in place, which, via the federal government budget in Berlin, make payments to support deficit regions. It is then the case that regional differences are called regional problems rather than balance-of-payments problems within a federal republic. They therefore show up as higher unemployment rates and lower average living standard for, without federal transfers, unemployment would be higher and living standards lower in regions with a 'trade deficit'.

Hence, even within a federal state, certain regions are poor because they have a weak trade balance. One part of the trade deficit within these poorer regions is often covered by remittances sent back home from relatives and emigrant workers being employed outside the region. Ultimately, some intermediate relief can be obtained by borrowing outside the region at a relatively high rate of interest or by some direct investments often subsidised by the federal government.

The differences in prosperity between the north and south of Italy or Eastern and Western Germany clearly demonstrate internal balances-of-payments imbalances, which are partly levelled out by federal transfer mechanisms. However, no such transfer schemes exist in relation to the workings of the EMU. If the private sector (typically private banks) or the public sector (the government) has an accumulated *foreign* debt, then they are at the mercy of foreign creditors and capital markets; that is to say, there are no automatic fiscal or social transfer mechanisms.

Therefore, surplus at the balance of payments and an international creditor position have a high priority to all countries and especially to countries without a national currency. Developing countries learned this lesson the hard way in the 1980s and South-East Asia in the late 1990s, although they still had their own currency and could therefore retain national sovereignty in economic policy.

Besides, on a global scale, it is a logical impossibility that all countries can have a balance-of-payments surplus. Indeed, this is hardly possible within a monetary union and could only happen if the entire Eurozone managed to establish an external balance-of-payments surplus, which is shared by all members. However, this is rather unlikely as long as more than 80 % of 'foreign' trade by Euro countries is within the EMU (Fig. 4.1).

As we can see from Fig. 4.1, the 2015 surplus was larger than ever within the consolidated current account of the Eurozone. This improvement was caused by the low value of the euro at the time, due to an expansionary monetary policy by the ECB (see Chap. 7) and a continued stagnation within the Eurozone, making the quantity of imports extraordinarily small, together with reduced energy prices.

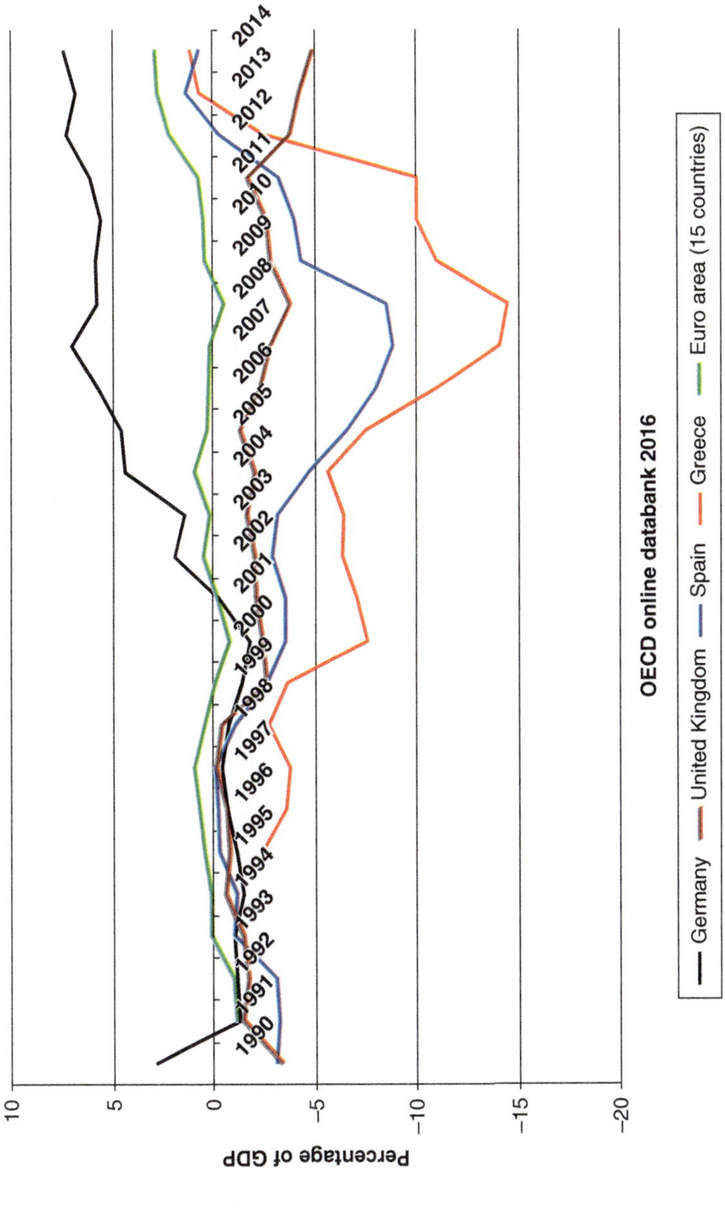

Fig. 4.1 Balance of payments (Percentage of GDP)

Source: OECD, Economc Outlook, 2016

WHY BALANCE-OF-PAYMENTS *IM*BALANCES ALWAYS MATTER

Within a monetary union, member countries become particularly dependent on each other in renouncing the use of their national currency and through the effect one country's use of a number of national instruments of economic policy, such as the central bank's lending rate and the exchange rate has on the other countries within the monetary union. The consequence is that, in regard to competition, individual countries cannot protect their industries from the aggressive policies of other member countries. Hence, to make the EMU work in practice, without any automatic transfer mechanism to counterbalance (a part of) the deficits, there should have been a legally binding agreement written into the Stability Pact, setting a maximum size of balance-of-payment *surplus* (and deficit) vis-à-vis the other member states.

Before the EMU was established, deficit countries could, if necessary, defend themselves against an aggressive German low-cost policy by devaluating their currency. By the time that the common currency was accepted, this possibility had disappeared. However, the negative macro-economic implications of a balance-of-payments deficit had not gone away. As we have already mentioned, persistent balance-of-payments deficits caused increasing tensions between the countries for at least two major reasons.

First, we should consider that a deficit in the current account is a direct measure of how much the foreign debt will grow, which has then to be financed abroad in addition to the servicing of the already existing debt (interest and amortisation). Hence, the private and/or public sector has to borrow this extra money abroad. The only way to pay back this increasing sum of borrowed money in the future is by a current account surplus. The big, unsolved question is then how such a change from deficit to surplus will ever be realised as long as the surplus countries keep their superior competitive position. In such a situation of deadlock, the only way to create a surplus is by reducing imports through deflationary policies.

Second, the correction of an unsustainable current account deficit causes loss of output and jobs. As such, the correction of an unsustainable current account deficit within a monetary union is both highly difficult to achieve and has substantial consequences for the domestic economy of the deficit countries.

The notion that international trade is to the benefit of all participating countries relies upon the assumption of balanced trade; when jobs are lost in some industries, they are gained in other sectors and the increased productivity is shared by the participating countries. This process has proved to be of mutual benefit due to policies enabling specialisation and the division of labour, which have improved productivity within the participating countries. If larger disturbances occur, then imbalances could quite easily be corrected via the foreign exchange rate. However, within a currency union, a persistent current account deficit is much more difficult to correct without supportive cooperation from the surplus countries.

Without agreed 'rules of the game' within a monetary union, a situation with persistent surpluses (and therefore persistent deficits) could easily result in a competition for cost-deflating wages, that is, a race to the bottom between the countries as regards deflation of wages to achieve increased competitiveness. In the 1930s, the international threat was 'competing devaluations'. These days, the threat is that of competing money wage reduction draining the Eurozone of purchasing power and effective demand.

Unfortunately, any effective limits on balance-of-payments surpluses are still missing, being that a binding requirement within the EU Treaty founding the EMU[1] and the Stability Pact (and presently the Fiscal Compact, see Chap. 6) is blocking a coordinated expansionary policy.

What Is a 'Structural Current Account'?

Developments on an EMU member's current account are dominated by three macroeconomic phenomena: (1) The relative cost level vis-à-vis the other EMU countries, (2) The output gap (positive or negative) and (3) The level of accumulated foreign wealth (positive or negative).

1. **Relative cost level**. Usually, this only concerns the development in relative *unit labour cost* (UCL), which is presented and analysed as a measurement of the inter-European competitive position of each country. Thus, an index of the relative wage costs is one part of the story behind the development of each country's current account.
2. **(Relative) output gap**. Equally important is the (relative) output gap between the EMU countries. Due to the dependence of imports on domestic output and consumption, a booming country

will typically run a deficit, whereas a recession country will show a surplus.

3. **Foreign debt** has to be serviced by interest payments (and mortification), and, in a longer-term perspective, the surplus of the current account.

All too frequently, the international competitive position is measured only by the development in the relative cost level, corrected for exchange rate changes when relevant. However, many other macroeconomic parameters play a significant role at home and abroad.

It is the opinion of this author that a measurement of a *structural current account* should be defined and calculated for each participating country. The definition of a *structural current account* comes quite close to balance of foreign trade in goods and services at full employment, corrected for net interest and dividend payment. Before the calculation can be made, three very delicate questions have to be answered.

1. What kind of macroeconomic model is used for this calculation? (Euro-monetarist or Euro-realist?)
2. How is full employment assumed to be established? (Through the expansion of public or private effective demand?)
3. What are we to assume with regard to the output gaps of European trading partners, particularly with other members of the currency union?

The answers to these questions will not be dealt with in detail here, but are taken up again in more detail in Chap. 5, and in Jespersen, 2016, where a calculation of a *structural public sector budget deficit* is discussed.

Those countries with a structural current account deficit have a problem because they cannot close their output gap without increasing the foreign debt, unless they improve their cost-competitiveness. Moreover, the said countries have to do it quicker than the other members of the monetary union, otherwise their interest repayments will increase. To correct the structural current account deficit, an improvement is needed of relative competitiveness within the monetary union. However, this requirement will apply to a number of countries simultaneously, which could easily trigger a race to the bottom of money wages.

Therefore, a calculation of the *structural balance of payments* could place the spotlight on those member countries with a permanent surplus. These are the states causing the deadlock and the risk of a race-to-the-bottom wage reduction in the deficit countries. Therefore, surplus countries within a monetary union should be legally committed to reducing their trade surpluses and, so, transferring a part of their excess surplus to a mutual investment fund or a euro clearing bank (either as direct transfers or as interest-free lending). It is thus crucial to create an institutional economic incentive to make surplus countries responsible for the smooth functioning of the monetary union in order to avoid tensions building up.

A much needed starting point for future reforms of the EMU would then be to focus on these excessive current account surpluses run by Germany, the Netherlands and Luxembourg, an approach similar to the Stability Pact (SP) directed at public sector budgets that we will discuss in Chap. 5. A structural current account should be balanced or, even better, the accumulated foreign wealth of these countries should be reduced to stabilise the working of the EMU. A structural surplus is obviously a burden on the trading partners and should therefore be reduced quickly. If such a reduction is not imposed, then a kind of legal fine (like excessive deficits in the SP) should be exercised in these countries. One way to avoid such a fine would be to increase the wage rate (UCL) to bring the cost level of the surplus countries to the euro average to avoid wage deflation (or, even better, above this average for a while).

However, without a legally binding principle on surplus countries, the European community will cease to have a mutual interest in a common currency and national policies will start to drift apart. In fact, one can see in the statistics that this development was under way right from the very beginning. Cost levels and balance of payments grew very differently in the north compared to the south, with France somewhere in between (see Fig. 6.1). However, no EU institution has taken notice of this trend and legal requirements have instead been concentrated on public sector deficit, which has put Germany and France in the limelight and derailed the policy requirements/recommendations away from the balance of payments.

In fact, what would have been required as regards the German economy in the early years of the EMU was an expansionary policy to reduce unemployment at home and at the same time to reduce the German balance-of-payments surplus. This policy could have helped deficit countries, particularly if they had also received a cost warning.

However, the trust in the market mechanism and the self-correcting private economy was dominant amongst economists, the EU Commission and a number of heads of government. This prevented a realist view on the consequences of persistent balance-of-payments deficits *and* surpluses from making an impact on actual policy making.

Box 4.1 Balance of payments: 'It's the current account that matters'

The argument has often been presented that the balance-of-payments problem would disappear when countries have the same currency.

This argument is clearly wrong; the need for foreign borrowing does not disappear, only the exchange rate risk, which is, itself, not certain. The calculation might become simpler as long as a 'Euro is a Euro', but it does not solve the problem of how to finance a current account deficit at the macro level.

The current account measures the income flows in and out of the country regardless of what currency revenues are registered. The currency is the only a unit of account, what matters is whether the current account is showing a surplus or a deficit. In terms of book-keeping, the current account also mirrors the positive or negative grain on liquidity; but here the capital account, measuring net borrowing abroad comes into play. The final settlement of the current account can be temporarily postponed through borrowing abroad. However, the final payments, which set the foreign account definitely, have to be via a positive current account.

The accepted means of payments are usually defined by international or national law (or, in more primitive societies, by convention). They can be gold coins, euro notes, private bank deposits or even objects such as seashells, dependent on law or social convention.

Let us now provide a few representative illustrations of 'balance-of-payments' imbalances – that is, income accounts imbalance under different circumstances – which are present and relevant between persons, regions within a country, or sovereign countries.

1. A deficit in the balance-of-payments current account has to be financed

If we were to look at the balance of payments (the book-keeping account of income-generating transactions) between two people named Robinson Crusoe and Friday, then whom would we say incurs debt to whom? If Robinson buys more coconuts from Friday than he can immediately pay for with seashells (perhaps because of high tide), then he must enter into a debt to Friday. Thus, Robinson commits himself on payments to Friday and must generate income in the future (he may hope that the mussels return to the seashore) in order for him to be able to meet his obligations. However, the longer this balance-of-payments deficit and debt lasts, the more dependent Robinson becomes upon Friday accepting a postponement of payment in cash (extending credit) and the greater the accumulated debt (which in real life causes interest payments).

Hence, in order to change the situation, Robinson must start to produce something that Friday wants to buy. If he does so, then Robinson could start to accumulate a surplus in his current account and thereby start repaying the accumulated debt. However, if it is the case that Robinson is not successful in selling more to Friday, then his other choice is to 'tighten his belt' and start to consume less coconuts (or learn to climb the palm trees to collect coconuts himself). This 'literary' metaphor hence illustrates the balance-of-payments problems right down to the individual level, which is also illustrative of the regional or the national level.

In addition, this can be illustrated using a Danish example. Denmark is divided into a number of regions. Some of them are pretty small and remote, such as the isle of Bornholm in the middle of the Baltic Sea. The people of Bornholm live off fishing, agriculture and tourism. The export side of their balance of payments consists of two export items (fish and tourism). When the cod catch fails, people living on Bornholm immediately run into balance-of-payments difficulties and cannot pay their usual import of consumer goods; they hence rely on resources from the fishing industry and agriculture. In this satiation, they then have to borrow 'abroad' to maintain imports and living standards. This does not happen automatically, being that it depends on banks in Copenhagen continuing to consider firms and private banks at Bornholm to be creditworthy.

For Bornholm, the longer the crisis drags on, the larger 'foreign' debt is accumulated the more the island's creditworthiness will be eroded and the more difficult it will be to finance the balance-of-payments deficit. Unemployment starts to rise because farmers cannot access the required level of imported feeding for cattle and pigs, as well as fertilisers, which begins a vicious cycle. Fortunately, Bornholm is a part of a federal structured economy, where a number of interregional safety nets are built into the legislation. For instance, unemployment benefits are paid by the central government, while Danish regions have interregional equalisation funds to support poorer regions. Moreover, schemes guaranteeing private bank deposits are organised at the national level, ensuring that banks at Bornholm do not experience an instantaneous run on the banks. Finally, the Danish parliament can make the decision of whether to establish a specific 'Bornholm package' with special funds for restructuring the fish industries, supporting tourism and setting up new companies (for instance, the sweets manufactured in Bornholm have become a great success).

However, it should not be overlooked that, in the end, Bornholm will have to create a surplus in its regional balance of payments, which will cause a fall in living standards compared to the Danish average. The number of people living at Bornholm will then fall as a consequence of emigration. The last slaughterhouse on the island was only saved from being closed by a last minute emergency loan from Copenhagen.

The overall point is that no household, no firm, no region and no nation can live with a permanent current account deficit because it needs to be financed by borrowing (or selling off assets if any are available). Borrowing is the usual solution, but one that cannot continue forever; this possibility dries up when creditworthiness is eroded. Creditworthiness is the key concept in any financial relationship, defined and supported by economic trust, institutional and legal commitments.

Theoretical Interlude: Do Not Mistake Foreign Debt for Public Debt!

Even among professors in economics and political science it is often the case that the concepts of foreign and public debt are not separated consistently and clearly.

In some ways, Euro-monetarists can be excused for confusing these two concepts. Their analytical models and economic arguments take for granted that the private sector is in equilibrium or tend to be so through financial savings being equal to real investment. Within these general equilibrium models, an imbalance of the public sector is mirrored directly by a similar balance-of-payments imbalance. We may recall that the so-called twin-deficit (public sector and balance of payments) serves as a causal relationship. It is the public sector imbalance which then causes a similar balance-of-payments imbalance within this theoretical approach. Thus, if the government balances its public finance, then the balance-of-payments deficit will disappear by itself – *deus ex machina.*

In contrast, Euro-realists make their case by looking at the numbers. Here, they draw on the manifold cases where private sector financial savings exceed private real investment, and so, may cause a recession and increased unemployment. In a closed society, when the private sector has excess savings, it must let conventional book-keeping principles spill over into an equally sized public sector deficit. In an open economy, however, when foreign trade is possible, the excess private sector financial savings may either be counterbalanced by balance-of-payment current account surplus and/or by the public sector deficit.

Germany is an archetypal example of private sector excess savings spilling over primarily into a balance-of-payments surplus and, to a minor extent, into public sector deficit (see Table 4.1).

Box 4.2 The foreign and public debts are very different

As we can see in Table 4.1, in round numbers, Germany's accumulated foreign assets correspond to the external debt of the three largest Eurozone countries. The reason is that the EMU countries as a whole (where the big four countries account for about 80 % of GDP) have a balance of foreign trade. Germany has a net export out

Table 4.1 Accumulated foreign and public debt, 1998–2014

Bill. Euro	*Priv. fin. wealth*	*Foreign wealth*	*Public debt*
France	1673	25	1648
Germany	3260	1940	1320
Italy	2030	-147	2177
Spain	244	-647	891

Note: Private Financial Wealth = Foreign Wealth + Public Debt
Source: OECD, Economic Outlook, June 2016

of the Eurozone which, until very recently, was counterweighted by the net import of the other Euro countries (from China and the United States, among others). The Eurozone equilibrium is partly a consequence of the euro exchange rate being floating at the international currency markets, that is, all the important trading partners ($, £, Yen, etc.), thereby offsetting major imbalances between imports and exports.

The floating euro exchange rate has made the Eurozone function more like a closed economic system, like Fig. 4.2. Thus, the most successful exporting country/ies benefit(s) from an income and employment generation at the expense of the other countries. A surplus of one Euro country will tend to be matched by an equivalent deficit in the current account of one or several of the other member states.

In practice, it means that as long as Germany maintains her current account surplus through targeted policies enhancing competitiveness, then euro-deficit countries cannot reduce their deficits. The deficit countries in the Eurozone have hence made themselves hostages of the policy pursued in Germany or, rather, hostages of the policy of all the surplus countries. The deficit countries can hardly improve their situation through savings on public budgets, being that public expenditure only has a modest effect on the import of goods from abroad. They thus experience a persistent current account deficit unless they deflate their economy substantially.

Public Debt = Private Financial Wealth

The private sector/public sector relationship of a closed society is illustrated in Fig. 4.2. Private financial surplus is, by definition, equivalent to the public sector deficit. The interesting question is what is cause and what is effect, to which there is no simple answer, for it depends on circumstances. Hence, as we will see next, with regard to the interpretation of the macroeconomic impact of a public sector deficit, it really matters to detect the chain of causality in reality.

Euro-monetarists assume within their models that the private sector is self-adjusting and is successful in obtaining an equilibrium between savings and investment at full employment. In this case, a structural public sector budget deficit is politically forced upon the private sector with the consequence of crowding out private real investment. The conclusion to be drawn in such cases is that the public deficit is a burden on the private sector due to smaller private investment.

Euro-realists, on the other hand, do not accept the claim that the private sector is able to balance its books due to the working of a (perfect) market system. In a number of countries including Germany,

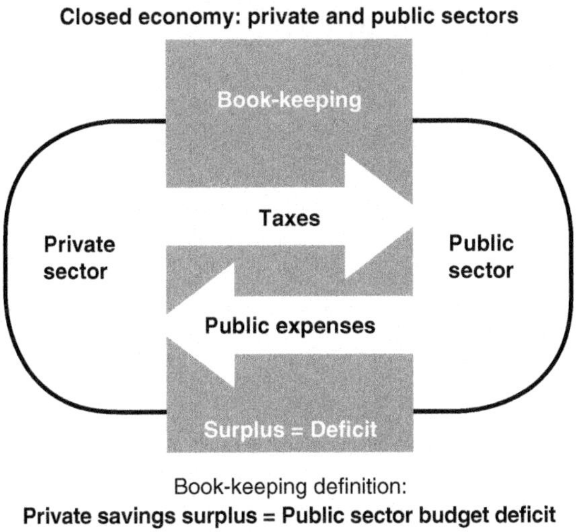

Fig. 4.2 A consolidated economic model: book-keeping entities

private financial savings (at full employment) would have exceeded real investment for decades. There has consequently been a lack of demand within the domestic economy when private savings exceed private real investments. This happens when private households and firms save without undertaking real investment at an amount needed for creating effective demand equivalent to full employment. In ages of uncertainty, private savings search for safe havens and therefore prefer to 'invest' in government bonds (or abroad). The reduced demand for real investments hence causes unemployment, which is a burden on society in the form of lost production, that is, an hour of unemployment is lost forever. The public sector can prevent that loss, for instance, by undertaking real investment in infrastructure. In this case, society will, for instance, receive an improved railway network, houses for refugees or windmills, and become wealthier than it otherwise would have been, when people stay unemployed.

Foreign Debt = Accumulated Current Account Deficits = Lack of Domestic Savings

Within a monetary union, a current account deficit means a loss of liquidity, because the government cannot print its own money. The sovereign state has become less sovereign. As long as the current account deficit goes on, foreign debt accumulates. There is a persistent lack of private and/or public savings. In such cases, it becomes increasingly difficult to get foreign loans at reasonable terms. Hence, one should separate the analysis of the consequences of a public sector deficit between countries with a surplus and those with a deficit within a monetary union. Surplus countries have a much easier case. They can borrow domestically and usually at a lower rate of interest, cf. the German and Dutch cases.[2]

1. A current account surplus implies that private banks and pension funds have excess liquidity, then it becomes easier for the government to sell bonds domestically.
2. A current account deficit implies that the private sector cannot finance the entire public sector deficit. In such cases, the government has to rely partly on foreign borrowing at a higher cost.

Hence, it is the accumulated foreign deficits, rather than the public deficits, which may cause severe financial difficulties and increased borrowing costs. The more the foreign debt accumulates, then the more obvious it becomes that the country has a structural balance-of-payments problem; hence, borrowing abroad becomes more expensive for private firms and public institutions. Thus, it makes quite a difference, whether there is a structural surplus or a deficit on the balance of payments.

Foreign debt consists of money borrowed *outside* the country, which then has to be served. In the end, foreign debt is to be paid back by the net export of goods and services. This reduces a country's future domestic living standard and it is why foreign debt is known as a 'burden on future generations' (Fig. 4.3).

Let us look at what it means if we were now to include the foreign sector in the analytical model. The current account of the Balance of payments is determined primarily by the import and export of goods and services, along with net interest payments on foreign debt. As we have

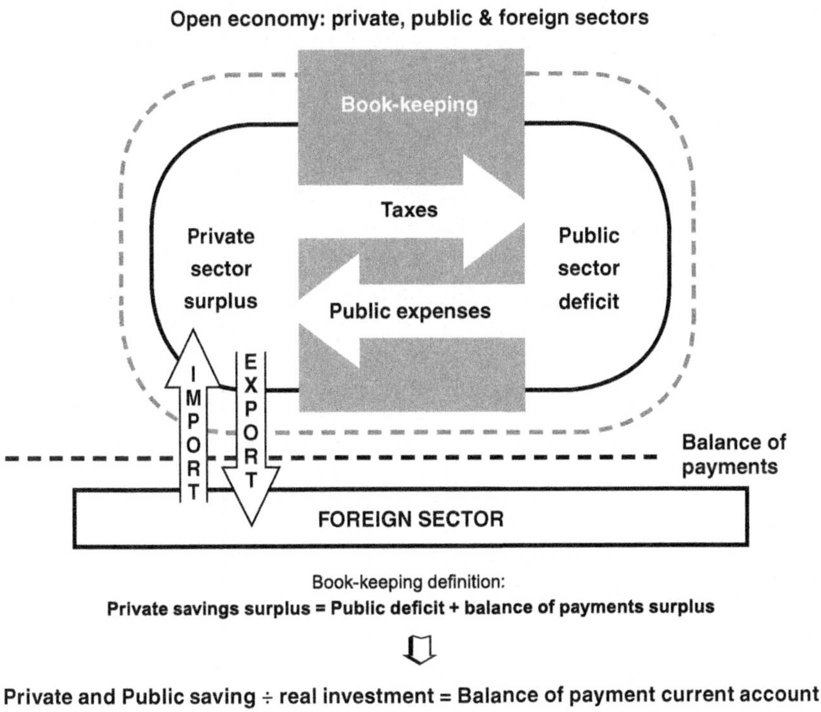

Fig. 4.3 A consolidated economic model: book-keeping entities

mentioned, the current account determines the country's additional borrowing requirements abroad.

A country's current account deficit means that the foreign debt grows. Hence, it is necessary to take out new loans abroad. The foreign borrowing requirement is independent of whether the country has its own currency or it is a member of a currency union. In both cases, it is a foreign bank, foreign finance company or pension fund which stands as the final creditor.

Conversely, a balance-of-payments surplus implies that, considered as a whole, the private sector (households, companies, pension funds and banks) and the public sector have a savings surplus. This surplus can be accumulated domestically (exchange reserves) or lent abroad if foreign debtors can provide attractive conditions.

However, financial institutions within a country with a current account surplus have no legal obligation to lend this surplus to deficit countries. This is the fundamental asymmetry, which has always marred fixed exchange rate systems and, hence, monetary unions with sovereign states, being that it creates political asymmetries. In such a scenario, creditor nations by definition become more powerful. They can keep their sovereignty unchallenged, whereas debtor nations quickly run into a position where they have to ask for more money with the 'cap in hand'.

Surplus countries do not have to lend to countries, which they consider to have a low credit rating. On the other hand, deficit countries must find a way to close the gap on their balance of payments. In the very real sense, they need international money because they cannot print themselves. This means that a deficit country will always have an urgent funding need that corresponds to the deficit on the current account. On top of this new borrowing requirement, the country concerned also needs foreign loans to make up for scheduled amortisation of their existing foreign debt.

Macroeconomic Disagreement

One can only understand why Euro-monetarists and Euro-realists disagree when the fundamental differences behind their analytical approaches are fully specified:

1. The Euro-monetarists assume full employment and a balanced private sector as normal in their analysis; while deviations – business cycles – are only considered as extraordinary and a short-term divergence from a long-term growth trend.[3]

2. Euro-realists take an analytical departure from *reality*, where excessive unemployment has been the regular situation in Europe since the 1970s (see the following Fig. 6.1). Therefore, it seems quite unrealistic to assume full (or near-full) employment as the normal situation. The private sector is measured by past historical development, which, clearly, is not self-adjusting. This has consequences for macro imbalances related to the public sector, but it even has ramifications when the balance of payments is under consideration. The balance of payments is the outcome of activities occurring simultaneously in the private sector of several countries but without self-adjustment mechanisms. The macroeconomic analysis has to be open-ended, and the assumption of actual full employment in practice makes no sense.

The Euro-monetarist view is dominant within the political and macroeconomic debate. It is the public deficit that is considered the economic problem due to excess public spending. The debate concentrates on how to balance the books of the public sector. Here, the consequences for employment are often disregarded (only considered as temporary).

If a realist approach was undertaken, then one would first ask: where and what are the roots of imbalance – in the private or public sector? This is not an easy question to answer convincingly. Second, unemployment has then to be considered, followed by the structural current account and finally public sector finances. If the origin of the macroeconomic imbalance is excess financial savings within the private sector, then policies should be directed towards rebalancing the savings/investment relationship, which is substantially different from policies aiming to correct public sector overspending.

Conclusion: EMU – An Unhappy Marriage between Surplus and Deficit Countries

The growing imbalance in the EMU countries' balance of payments (distinct from the budget balance) has revealed that the twelve countries did not in any respect constitute an 'optimal' currency area in the beginning. This conclusion is obvious to anyone who has analysed the development of the countries' relative competitiveness and growing current account imbalances. However, no official concern was expressed; not even after the nature of the financial and economic crisis became apparent to everyone. Private banks were rescued, while governments were blamed for not having controlled their public sector budget.

Of course, there are clear differences amongst EMU countries. Some governments had run a structural public sector deficit even though their private sector was booming and this had contributed to the mounting current account deficit. However, this development went unnoticed all the way through to the 2007/08 financial crisis.

These arguments tell a story of how political rhetoric – 'the single currency is good for European cooperation' – has gone hand in hand with the euro-optimism involved in idealising generalised market models, with perfect financial sectors providing credit wherever it is needed. Yet, macroeconomic realities, that is, increasing differences in cost levels and current account imbalances, were neglected in the official discussions. Instead, the focus was exclusively on the deficit in public sector budgets, due to the requirements stated in the Stability and Growth Pact. However, such imbalances are of secondary importance when getting a monetary union to function.

Instead, it is the persistent denial amongst both politicians and Euro-monetarists that 'the Euro is the problem', which has caused the Euro area to under-perform compared to the United States and the non-Euro countries within the EU.

Notes

1. As a consequence of the economic crisis within the EU, it was realised in 2011 that it is not only an imbalance at the public sector budget which might cause a prolonged recession. Other macroeconomic imbalances also matter. Hence, a macroeconomic score board for each individual country was set up containing twelve criteria for macroeconomic imbalance; one of them is a balance-of-payments surplus (6 per cent of GDP) and deficit (3 per cent of GDP). Hereby, it is demonstrated that the EU Commission, which has designed the score board, still has not understood the interconnectedness of balance-of-payments surpluses and deficits within the EU, not to speak of the importance of ensuring that Germany (and other countries with persistent surplus) remains committed to reducing its huge surplus running annually at a level of € 200 billion.
2. This conclusion also holds for countries with their own currency, cf. Japan, Switzerland, Denmark – I leave this argument aside for the moment.
3. See, Mankiw (2016).

CHAPTER 5

Public Sector Deficit and Debt: Cause or Effect?

Abstract Euro-monetarists assume the private sector to be self-adjusting. Therefore, persistent macroeconomic imbalances have to be rooted in disequilibrating policies, which manifest themselves in public sector deficits. Euro-monetarists consider business cycles as short term and as minor deviations from the growth trend. The effect of automatic stabilisers should only be accepted within the 3 percent budget limit codified in the Stability Pact.

In reality, the private sector is not self-adjusting. Excess savings have, especially after 2008, become common place in most Euro countries, causing the automatic budget deficit to increase far beyond 3 percent. In this way, austerity policy has in many countries increased unemployment without significantly reducing the public sector debt ratio.

Fiscal policy is relevant to stabilise the economy considered as a whole.

Keywords Unemployment causing public sector budget deficit · Private sector excess saving · Lack of self-adjustment · Persistent macroeconomic imbalance · Fallacy of composition

Some Introductory Remarks

This chapter has been the most difficult to write and probably to read. I shall elaborate here on why the different theoretical perspectives on the 'economy as a whole' are decisive to draw conclusions on the causes and consequences of 'public sector deficit and debt'. Even more challenging is

J. Jespersen, *The Euro*, DOI 10.1007/978-3-319-46388-9_5

the fact that only a correct understanding can change the failures of the EMU and secure a prosperous economic future of *the EU as a whole*.

Thus, we, the Europeans, are confronted with the intellectual challenge of understanding how a monetary union functions in practice and the role played by public sector economics, independently of ideology. This is a difficult exercise, because until the euro crisis evolved, there was only one theory in town – euro-monetarism. When the rationality of the EMU occasionally was on the agenda, all governments of the Eurozone, independently of whether they were left- or right-leaning promoted the common currency using Euro-monetarist arguments. So, as we have seen the main, not to say sole, argument, for making the EMU work properly was to ensure a balanced public budget.

However, reality tells a different story: public deficits are common practice. Why, at least until recently, does reality run counter to the recommendations offered by the macroeconomic theory that has generally been accepted? Why are there so often deficits in public budgets? In the eyes of the Euro-monetarists, the answer is simple. Politicians might be driven by self-interest to spend public money to buy voters and to promote re-election.

Such 'rational' political behaviour makes it necessary for cool-headed economists to recommend constitutional restrictions on the politicians' use of public money. We see it in the call for an *independent central bank* and a *limit on public sector deficits* in all the EU member countries. These requirements are implemented in the EU Treaty and are applicable to all EU member states. Being a member of the Eurozone makes these rules more binding. If public sector budget rules are not respected, then the EU Commission can recommend that a number of fines be imposed and that the ECB stop providing lending facilities to the banks concerned.

Hence, Euro-monetarism has defined the 'rules of politics' with regard to public finances and monetary policy (Chap. 7). What are the consequences when Euro-realities differ from the macroeconomics of euro-monetarism?

Public Finances Are a Part of 'the Economy as a Whole'

From a socio-economic perspective, it will be necessary to view the entire macroeconomic system as a whole (or 'the economy as a whole'). In other words, government budget deficit cannot be analysed in isolation from the rest of the economy.

Purely accounting principles tell us that a deficit has to be matched by a surplus of exactly the same size elsewhere in the economic system considered as a whole. This principle was highlighted in Chap. 4 with regard to the balance of payments. When the public sector has a deficit, there must, by definition, exist a surplus of equal size. The question is where? The answer is simple: the private sector(s).

Nonetheless, before going in search of the 'missing' surpluses, we need to discuss the causes and consequences of public deficits and private surpluses. It is only when the Euro-monetarists assume the private sector to be self-adjusting that this causality chain is 'one way'. In reality, it could be the imbalance between financial savings and real investment in the private sector that stands as a persistent cause and is consequently mirrored in the public sector (and/or the balance of payments). In such cases, a public deficit could better be understood and therefore analysed as the derived effect of a financial surplus in the private sector. It is analytically then a crucial matter to detect which direction causality will take; that is, the relationship is not, in reality, one way.

Therefore, from the perspective of causality and pluralistic macroeconomic theories, it is striking that this is the only concern connected to the public sector deficit and debt. The above dominated the political arguments when the institutional set-up was launched back in 1989 and did so again when the present euro crisis culminated in 2012. No one, in this prolonged period, really cared about other macroeconomic imbalances, such as the balance of payments, let alone unemployment. This is one reason why the euro has failed insofar as it has caused so much social distress without any serious attention from Brussels, Frankfurt or Berlin.

Are Politicians Guards of the Common Good?

From the perspective of Euro-monetarist theory, national politicians easily become the target for criticism when public deficits are on the agenda. Since the euro was introduced, such criticism has often been expressed by the EU's institutions, mainstream economists and by 'unionists'. These arguments were made explicit as paragraphs in the EU Treaty and considered as preconditions for securing the success of the euro and economic development or prosperity within the Eurozone countries. They have been repeated by almost every stakeholder in and around Brussels (EU Commission) and Frankfurt (ECB) while the argument remains monotone: it is not the euro which causes the problems, but Euro governments failing to balance their budgets. Hence, the success of the euro relies heavily on the institutional framework to ensure that governments restrict their public sector deficit and constantly aim for a balanced budget. As we have seen, this has been a part of the original convergence criteria (Treaty of Maastricht), the added Stability Pact (Treaty of Amsterdam) and, lately, when the crisis had unfolded, the even stricter Fiscal Compact (not yet incorporated into the EU Treaty).

This single-minded focus on the public sector and a balanced public budget demonstrates that the fathers of the EMU did not only have pure economic arguments on their agenda. They did, of course, know that there was more than one macroeconomic tale in town. However, only the Euro-monetarists were considered to be 'politically correct' in EU terms and became the academic fig-leaf supported by the populist argument that 'one market needs only one currency'. Hence, the Euro-monetarists' arguments have also become an intellectually respectable way to discipline the use of public finances by left-leaning politicians. The same academic arguments have provided the undercurrent behind the Euro-monetarist requirement of making the European Central Bank independent of the political decision-making process.

Euro-monetarists seem, through their models, not to trust politicians as guards of the common good. Using theoretical arguments which take individual optimisation as a behavioural axiom, it is not surprising that monetarists fear that politicians are also maximising their self-interest rather than the common good. I have always wondered about the aforementioned – why have these suspicious on the part of many conventional economists been directed at the politicians and not the economists themselves? How can it be that economists feel themselves to be elevated above self-interest? In defence of the monetarist view, it has to be said that hardly any politician within the Brussels elite has objected to this view – not even the socialist government. However, I will leave this thought aside until the very conclusion of this chapter.

Here, I want only to investigate the macroeconomic consequences of imposing strict rules on public sector finances within the EMU.

As explained in the previous chapters, when macroeconomic instability increases as a consequence of adopting a common currency in a non-optimal environment, what role should the public sector and fiscal policies adopt in serving as a stabilising counterweight? Should they hereby act to reduce the risk of the failure of the Euro?

Fallacy of Composition (I): 'You Can't Live Beyond your Means'

It is common practice on the part of Euro-monetarists to use housekeeping arguments within the sphere of macroeconomic reasoning. Indeed, it is a popular approach to win the argument in a political contest by claiming: 'As all of us know from our own household experience, one cannot go on living beyond one's own means. So, what counts for the individual should also count for the government. Therefore, the public sector budget should be balanced, if not every year then as an average over the short term business cycle'.

For people who have not studied macroeconomics, this argument appears correct, if not trivial, at least. Yet macroeconomists studying the economy as a whole should know better. In reality, the macroeconomic outcome cannot be deduced only from the idealised behaviour of individuals, assuming that macroeconomic behaviour has been described by just one representative rational agent (i.e. self-optimising) with rational expectations (i.e. perfect foresight). Although individuals are assumed to behave rationally, their aggregate activity has to take into account diversity and interaction, while, of course, perfect foresight is outside the realm of realism (see Jespersen 2009).

As a macroeconomist, you have to apply reason to figure out what, in reality, is likely to occur in the economy as a whole. Individual behaviour takes place within the private sector, while the outcome of the economic activities of the private sector is determined by millions of households, that is, wage earners (who spend and save), firms, entrepreneurs (who produce and undertake real investment) and financial institutions (providing money and credit). Within a modern, globalised economic environment, there is no *a priori* reason to believe that these millions of decisions taken individually should end up making the private sector in each country secure full resource utilisation, that is, full employment and a stable financial environment.

As we have already seen in Chap. 4, when there is a mismatch between demand and supply, and where savings are larger than real investment within the private sector, this imbalance has to spill over into an unbalanced public sector budget (and/or a balance-of-payments imbalance). In the end, this indisputable notion of book-keeping is derived from the national accounting system, where the sum of all surpluses and deficits within the economic system as a whole has to add to zero.

If the private sector cannot be expected always to match its intended financial savings with real investment at full employment, there will be a lack of effective demand, which a deficit at the public budget may counterweight and thereby act as a kind of real economy stabiliser. Fortunately, the built-in automatic stabilisers (related to welfare state arrangements) is doing a part of this job, preventing the fall of demand to some extent.

However, in such cases, any predetermined limit with regard to the size of the public sector deficit set too narrowly could have a destabilising effect on the private sector, causing more unemployment and a prolonged recession.

This represents one set of macroeconomic imbalances which does not occur by itself. In fact, out of fear and uncertainty, private household may start to increase savings and therefore impose a deficit on the public sector. From this realistic perspective it hardly makes sense to have a fiscal rule which requires that the public sector should also increase savings just to balance its books. The behaviour of 'double-saving' would only further destabilise the economy as a whole.

There are many other instances of fallacies of composition in macroeconomics. For instance, when it is argued that macroeconomic outcomes can be derived from a simple aggregation of individual (micro)economic behaviour analysed with a general equilibrium framework. Such a fallacy could sound like: 'There is a job for everyone, who is willing to accept the market determined wage rate.' The Euro-monetarists express it slightly differently: 'The supply of labour creates its own demand' (i.e. full employment arrives by itself). This fallacy is well known in neoclassical macroeconomics; here it is called Say's Law.

It is correct that one person may reduce his/her wage claim to take a job, but only at the expense of another wage earner. Moreover, this tends to happens when the number of jobs is limited. In such cases, two people swap their situation of employment and unemployment, but at the price of a lower wage income. Hence, the aggregate wage income available to be spent on the consumption good has been reduced. Finally, this may cause reduced demand for consumption goods, less production and more workers to be made redundant.

Fallacy of Composition (II): 'The Sun Is Moving Around the Earth'

Allow me to present another empirical parable to explain why, when arguments are applied to macroeconomic issues, the 'obvious' is not necessarily the 'real'. Anyone looking up the sky can see the sun is moving during the day from east to west, while this movement repeats itself next morning. In the Middle Ages, only a few scientists challenged the orthodoxy that the earth was at the centre of the universe with the sun revolving around it. That is to say, they dared to challenge the obvious and were therefore considered heretics which, to say the least, made life difficult for them. It took several hundred years and many, many careful empirical measurements before doubts arose.

The similarities to macroeconomics are striking. Macroeconomic phenomena cannot be observed directly. Only theoretical models of the economy as a whole, combined with skilful and careful use of econometric methods used on data from national accountancy, can reveal the most likely explanation of the macroeconomic dynamic forces. Indeed, the similarities to astronomy are striking. It was not until very precise predictions were made possible by the Newtonian planet model that the public and the Church were at last convinced that the sun were in the centre. Yet, macroeconomics is lagging far behind astronomy with regard to precise forecasts. In fact, macroeconomics will never be like (natural) sciences because social phenomena are 'man made' without any eternal laws of movement.

On the other hand, many macroeconomists have the aspiration to set up a model capable of giving reliable answers to what different policies and institutional reforms may bring in the future. A macroeconomic model is a system with many intertwined relationships at the national level and at the international level, where a common currency forces a far-reaching institutional change, which makes the consequences of fiscal rules deviate from past experiences.

For those governments that do not have an independent currency and central bank, the public sector budget – that is, fiscal policy – is almost the only tool which is left to stabilise the economy as a whole. Hence, it is even more crucial to understand the role of public debt and deficits correctly.

Let me now summarise the two sections on the 'fallacy of composition'. They have provided simple examples of why macroeconomic results cannot, in general, be derived from microeconomic arguments assuming individual optimisation and fully flexible and self-adjusting markets. These conclusions are important because they provide theoretical arguments as to why monetarism cannot, in most cases, provide a realistic understanding of macroeconomic dynamics in terms of the economic consequences of the public sector.

Different Concepts Related to the Public Sector Budget

To understand what we are referring to when speaking about the public sector, we have to navigate some rather dry definitions and concepts related to public sector finances, budget and debt. Having reached a decent level of understanding, we are ready to see the public sector as an integrated part of the 'economy as a whole'.

1. **Current public sector budget (deficit),** that is, public sector borrowing requirement: (expenses: public consumption, public real investment, social benefits and interest payments) minus (income/ revenue: taxes, consumer charges and privatisations). In fact, this includes all cash flows except financial transactions, and is the definition used when fulfilments of convergence criteria and the Stability Pact are considered. The sole focus here is on public sector borrowing requirement. If real sector activity were the main concern related to the public sector budget, then one would instead recommend a split between public consumption (continuous stream) and public investments (a one-shot effect). Likewise, social expenditure can be separated into a structural part related to, among other things, old age pensions and a varying part dependent on unemployment benefit and related to the business cycle of the specific year.

   The EU's convergence criteria and the Stability Pact limit the size of the current deficit at 3 percent of GDP – except for extraordinary cases with negative GDP growth.
2. **Primary public sector budget** is defined as the current budget, minus net interest payments. It is shorthand for the public sector's financial capacity to serve the already accumulated public debt without borrowing. For instance, a condition of the Troika (EU Commission, ECB and IMF) has been made to demand a considerable surplus of the Greek primary budget of 3½ percent of GDP.
3. **Automatic stabilisers** in regard to the budget refer to the social benefits caused by unemployment and to changes in tax revenues caused by the deviation of actual GDP from potential GDP. Automatic stabilisers will have a deteriorating effect on the budget, when unemployment is higher than the structural level and the output gap is positive (i.e. potential output larger than current output). The calculation is dependent on the macroeconomic model

and on the definition of structural unemployment and the potential output gap.

4. **Structural (underlying) budget** is the current budget corrected for the effect of automatic stabilisers. The outcome of the calculation is often interpreted as a measurement of the discretionary fiscal policy undertaken. A balanced structural budget is seen as a neutral fiscal policy, while a deficit and surplus are considered as an expansionary/contractive fiscal policy.

   The fiscal compact agreed upon by twenty-six EU member states has limited the size of the deficit to ½ percent of GDP at any time, independent of the size of the output gap. In practice, this means that expansionary fiscal policy is ruled out at any time, even when the output gap is considerable.

5. **Public sector financial gross debt** is the measurement over time of the aggregate public sector borrowing requirements in relation to current GDP. In the Stability Pact and the Fiscal Compact, the upper limit is set to 60 percent of GDP. Under normal conditions, GDP is expected to grow by, for instance, 4 percent each year, which means that the nominal public debt could also grow by 4 percent without any change to the debt/GDP ratio.

6. **'Sustainable public finances'** means that a longer-term perspective is taken on the development in public finances under consideration of changes in the demographic structure. In periods when the population grows older due to increased average life expectation, the labour force shrinks as a proportion of the population and public finances come under pressure. The question then to be asked is whether the public debt/GDP ratio will stay constant during a longer-term period, given the present tax rates and the norms and standards of public expenditures related to the welfare state.

Box 5.1 Summary of concepts related to public sector finances

1. Current budget: all tax income + revenue from the privatisation of public property – public consumption – public real investment – social expenditures – interest payments
2. Primary budget: current budget before payment of interest.
3. Structural budget: current budget corrected for the impact of the automatic stabilisers. (A change in the structural budget

can in principle only happen as a consequence of an *active* fiscal policy).

4. Primary structural budget: structural budget before payment of interest (considered as shorthand for the impulse from fiscal policy).
5. Sustainable budget: calculated of a structural budget, which could keep the public debt/GDP ratio constant in the long run taking demographic changes into consideration.

Public Sector and the 'Economy as a Whole'

The next question related to the public sector is: What are the statistical counterparts to the public sector? As we have already seen in Figs. 4.2 and 4.3, they are the private sector savings/real investment balance and the balance-of-payments current account. Within the national accounting system, these three sector balances add up to zero. This principle is then simple to demonstrate using the national accounting system.

Looking at Table 5.1 it becomes obvious that the private sector is not balancing its books. In fact, there has been a savings surplus in most cases over the past 20 years. Private real investment could not catch up with the potential private financial savings at full employment.

Moreover, equilibrium within the private sector is not only a matter of balance between savings and real investment. Low unemployment, low price inflation and the absence of a balance-of-payments deficit are even

Table 5.1 Private sector: excess savings

Percent of GDP	*1995*	*2000*	*2005*	*2010*	*2015*
France	5.9	2.5	3.2	6.0	3.4
Germany	8.2	–2.7	8.0	9.6	7.9
Italy	9.6	1.4	3.2	0.8	4.8
Poland	4.9	–3.3	1.4	2.1	2.4
Spain	6.1	–3.4	–8.7	5.5	6.5
United Kingdom	4.7	–3.4	2.3	6.9	–0.7
Euro area (15 countries)	7.7	–0.5	2.9	6.6	5.9

Source: OECD, Economic outlook, 2016

more important. We have already discussed these in the previous chapter, but unemployment and low inflation will be addressed in the next chapter.

Now, we will focus on the interrelationship between the private and public sectors, leaving the balance of payments aside. The main question is whether the two sectors are self-adjusting. If one sector can balance its saving/investment account by itself, then the other would be forced to have a balance budget.

We have already discussed the two different schools of macroeconomics and their fundamentally different theories in order to explain the origin of macroeconomic imbalances and the role of the public sector:

1. **Euro-monetarists** assume (and this is a pure assumption) that the private sector is self-adjusting. This is not an empirically proven theory, but a conclusion deducted and built on the axioms of rational individuals, of perfect foresight and of a well-behaved and competitive private market system. If these were to be the case, then the private sector would adjust to full employment and a saving/investment balance. Hence, within a macroeconomic system where the private sector is self-adjusting, it is only external events, originating from within other sectors, which can disturb the smooth development of the private sector. In this case, we would expect to see low figures of unemployment and a balanced private sector account.

However, we see by looking at Table 5.1 it is clearly not the case that the private sector has been in macroeconomic balance in any of the larger Eurozone member states. Nonetheless, according to the reasoning of the Euro-monetarists, these macroeconomic imbalances must be caused by a political mismanagement of public finances. In rarer cases, disturbances might originate in other sectors such as the financial sector (banking crisis) or the foreign sector (collapse of export markets). Hence, following the logic of the Euro-monetarist model, the short-circuit of the self-adjustment process in the private sector can be explained in terms of political activity that destabilises the private sector and the economy as a whole. This destabilising activity is registered statistically as deficits (and surpluses – but seldom mentioned) at the current and/or structural budget.

As mentioned earlier, the *structural budget* is a (rough) measurement of the destabilising effect of the aggregate public sector activities undertaken by a government. To prevent the politicians of this government opting for self-optimising and public expenditures to seek re-election instead of looking for the common good, the rules compel the government to balance the structural budget. According to the Fiscal Compact, the deficit must not be more than equal to ½ percent of GDP in any of the EU member states (where Great Britain and the Czech Republic are exempted). In practice, this limit means that EU countries are prevented from undertaking any significant expansionary policy even during the trough of the business cycle.

The agreed size of the *current budget deficit* is less restrictive. The maximum is 3 percent of GDP set by the EU Treaty and the Stability Pact. This leeway is made possible to allow the automatic stabilisers to 'work' during unavoidable business cycles caused by external shocks and short-term private sector misalignments. In rare cases where GDP falls by more than 1 percent, an even larger deficit may be accepted by the EU Commission if a credible plan for the reduction of the current budget deficit is put forward by the government of the deficit country.

In addition, a maximum limit has also been set for the acceptable size of the *public (gross) debt*. Here the upper limit is 60 percent of GDP. Indeed, not much attention had been devoted to this limit until the financial crisis swept the European countries. From the very beginning, EMU countries such as Italy, Belgium and Greece had public debt ratios far above this limit without any consideration being given to them. However, during the crisis, a number of the more conservative countries, Germany prominent amongst them, had to acknowledge that their debt ratio also exceeded the 60 percent limit, partly because their GDP fell(!) and the current deficit swelled to a level far above 3 percent(!).

The excesses outlined earlierabove have been recognised and addressed by the Fiscal Pact. Here the Pact requires that any public debt ratio exceeding 60 percent should be reduced each year by at least 2 percentage point; for instance, from 84 percent of GDP to 82 percent. Such a reduction of the ratio between the debt and GDP can be achieved either by growing GDP or by reducing the debt through a current budget surplus. Within monetarist reasoning, GDP will grow by itself (due to the self-adjustment assumption), reducing unemployment and improving the current budget. This adjustment will come by itself if politicians understand and restrict themselves to securing a balanced structural budget.

Finally, it has to be mentioned that within these fixed limits of the structural budget, the current budget and public debt ratio are arbitrarily chosen. There is no scientific explanation for this 'magic' size of ½ percent, 3 percent and 60 percent of GDP, or an explanation for why this number should be the right one permanently for all EU countries. This concept, if it is one at all, is built on the vision that all countries are alike and a 'one size fits all' approach is possible. This attitude which has been echoed within Bruxelles ever since the early 1990s, exemplified by the publication by the EU Commission of 'One market, One currency'.

Looking at the economy as a whole, one could ask: why has the balance of payments not been mentioned earlier by a single word? Two reasons can be given here. When the private sector has adjusted to equilibrium and where private financial savings equal real investment, then this is not considered as a theoretical, political or practical issue (whether or not these real investments have been undertaken domestically or abroad) because they are, by assumption, matched by private savings. If one country experiences a net outflow of direct investments, then it will automatically have a surplus at the current account, that is, it will have private savings larger than domestic real investment. If the public sector has a balanced budget, then these excess savings are channelled abroad via the capital account at the balance of payments. Similarly, if one country experiences a balance-of-payments deficit, then this is to be explained by individual actors' *rational* decisions to invest more than they save in the private sector.

Monetarists assume that the accompanying balance-of-payments surplus abroad is automatically re-circulated and made available to finance the excess of real investment.

This equalising mechanism is only broken in the monetarist model, if one country experiences a rise or fall in the demand for money, which is usually considered as a rare case. See, for instance, *The Monetary Approach to the Balance of Payments* by Johnson, which we will discuss further in Chap. 7.

2. Euro-realists: What do we know about the public sector and the economy as a whole? Here, we have to be cautious about determining what 'as a whole' mean? The Euro-monetarists look at one country at a time with focus only on the public sector budgets. Realists look at the entire economic system because no such thing as private sector equilibrium is assumed a priori, which, in fact, may be substantiated by examining Table 5.1.

In addition, countries which trade a lot and share the same currency cannot be analysed independently of each other. Instead, they are highly integrated via the balance of payment current and capital accounts. As we explained in Chap. 4, the current account registers real activity but mainly the export and imports of goods and services and interest payments abroad. All of the above have a derived impact on GDP, employment and real income in all the participating countries. Meanwhile, a surplus has an expansionary effect and a deficit the reverse. Therefore, all countries aim at a surplus, which, by definition, is not possible. However, this does not prevent countries from undertaking policies to improve the current account and, in doing so, become victims of the 'fallacy of composition'. The capital account of the balance of payments registers capital flows, where short-term financial flows have become the dominant part, given ample possibilities for speculative transactions destabilising the financial sector under attack.

Therefore, Euro-realists would ideally have to set up an interlinked model of all Eurozone countries split into at least three sectors: public, private and financial. Such a model has yet to be set up. However, the late Wynne Godley stock-flow modelling approach has been an important step in this direction. A number of post-Keynesian scholars in Greenwich, Berlin, Paris, Kingston and recently Aalborg have further elaborated a number of important ideas, see for instance Madsen and Olesen (eds) 2016. In the view of these studies, instead of assuming general equilibrium, the entire Eurozone is being analysed in a dynamic perspective and path-dependent process, where 'one size does not fit everyone'. In reality, countries are different and they develop differently through time, making macroeconomic imbalances differ, which can be seen in Table 5.1.

Taking the realists' view on the Eurozone then, there is no reason to assume that the private sector in each country should be self-adjusting. Persistent unbalancing effects derived from the private sector provide a mismatch between financial savings and real investment. These come from the balance-of-payments current account surpluses (in some countries) and deficits (in other countries), from the financial sector and, finally, from the public sector budget (which can also be destabilising as well as stabilising, depending on circumstances and policies).

In this chapter, we will focus upon the role of the public sector and fiscal policies, analysing the impact of the different budgets on macroeconomic development. Euro-monetarists and Euro-realists are in least disagreement about the working of the *automatic budget stabilisers*. From both perspectives, they perceive the stabilisation of private sector real activities during booms and troughs. However, the importance of the size of the stabilisers differs because they relate to welfare institutions designed by the politicians and therefore scrutinised with some scepticism by the monetarists. A social safety net consisting of unemployment benefit, high marginal income and consumption tax rates do serve to stabilise the macroeconomic system. At the same time, some economists claim that this causes a negative impact on individuals' incentive to supply labour and to undertake business initiatives. Monetarists then accuse the welfare state of making the economy smaller and less dynamic, which, for them, is an argument for recommending an upper limit on the current account of the public budget.

The Euro-realists would then counter-argue that some of the best-performing EU countries are those with the most extended welfare state institutions. The overall workings of the labour market cannot only be judged only by the individual economic incentives to work, that is, real disposable wage compared to social benefit. In relation to the labour market then, the overall institutional framework also makes a difference: generous social benefit and high marginal tax rates make disposable income more stable. The magnitude of these social phenomena is related to the welfare state ideology. There is also a different view with regard to the significance of inequality as Euro-realists recognise that the more equal societies are also the most harmonious, see Wilkinson and Pickett (2010).

With regard to fiscal policy, the two schools have opposing views. As we have seen, the Euro-monetarists recommend a neutral fiscal policy represented by a balance structural budget all the way through because of the a priori axiom of a self-adjusting private sector. Euro-realists cannot accept this axiom, which, according to their view, remains a theoretical 'special case' relying on the ideal assumption of individuals having perfect foresight and the market economic system being extremely well behaved; that is being attracted to a simultaneous/general equilibrium. As Table 5.1 shows, both assumptions cannot be supported or substantiated by empirical studies.

If the Euro-realist view is accepted, then there is an important case to be made for fiscal policy stabilising the private sector and the labour market, particularly within a closed economy where the balance of payments plays a minor role. Fiscal policy is a double-edged sword, being that unemployment and the balance of payments and the current account deficit all appear at the same time. It has been confirmed quite recently that fiscal policy is a (very) potent policy instrument, especially in recessions (see Guajardo et al. 2011, Ostry et al. 2016). The potential impact is even reinforced when more countries undertake fiscal contraction (or expansion) at the same time. As long as a single-country model has been used to calculate the economic impact, the effect has been underrated for three reasons: (1) No feedback effect from abroad, although a fiscal contraction in one country has a negative impact on trading partners' economic performance, (2) Reduced exports to neighbouring countries will increase unemployment and weakened public sector finances, and (3) current budget and balance of payments, which may call for fiscal consolidation. Hence, we are witnessing a vicious circle somewhat similar to the beggar thy neighbour policies undertaken in the 1930s.

Euro-realists have debated whether the best shorthand for the character of fiscal policy in one country is the structural budget or the primary structural budget. The OECD has recently calculated that if the primary structural budget is used, then the upshot is that, in the year 2014, the EU country with the most contractive fiscal policy was Greece and – surprise – the most expansionary fiscal policy was Great Britain!

One should also recall that, within the Eurozone, fiscal policy is the only demand management instrument which has been left to the member countries to decide upon. That is, it is fixed arbitrarily within narrow limits by the 'fathers of the Euro'.

Hence, public finance is not only a matter of the current budget where imbalances are mainly related to the working of the automatic stabilisers. If unemployment were to go away by itself, then most countries would have a balanced structural budget. Then, if interest payments were to go away (primary structural budget), most countries would still have a surplus today, see Fig. 5.1, that is, they would, by using this measure, clearly pursue a restrictive fiscal policy.

This should make us wonder: how can we be in a situation when unemployment is extraordinarily high, due principally to excess savings in the private sectors. Hence, is not fiscal policy supporting macroeconomic expansion by activating the excess private savings by real public investments? Is this not especially the case when we encounter the huge number of public projects required to improve infrastructures, durable energy, schools, hospitals and nursing homes, which unemployed people are ready to undertake. In any case, when unemployment benefit is paid, society gets nothing in return other than a good conscience. Finally, if unemployed people were to receive a proper job, then society as a whole would obtain a real investment for future use.

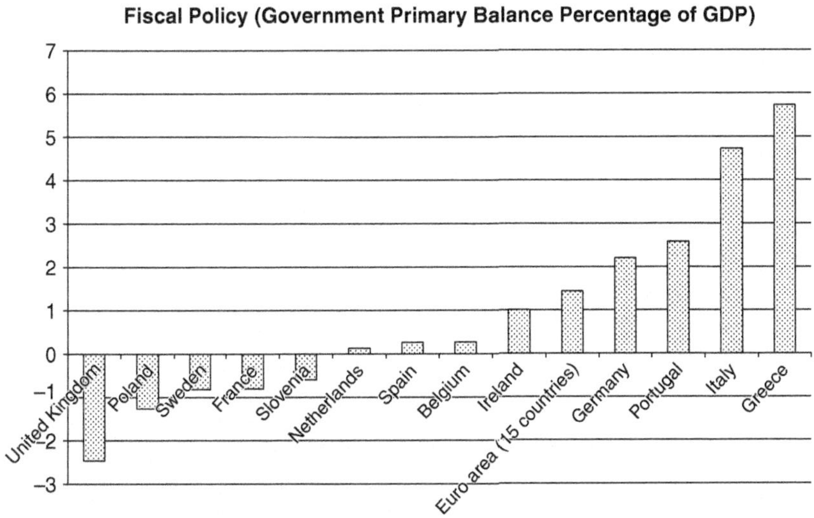

Fig. 5.1 Fiscal policy: Underlying primary budget, 2014

Note: I have a number of reservations related to the practice of OECD uses to calculate the underlying public budget (underestimating the output gap).[1] Even with this reservation in mind, it is telling that the Eurozone as a whole undertakes a restrictive fiscal policy, while unemployment is still above 10 percent of the labour force.

Source: OECD, Economic Outlook, 2016

Spain: A Telling Case of Macroeconomic Causality

Spain is a telling case of why the single-minded focus at the public sector deficit has led to an understanding of macroeconomic imbalances (and risks) astray. When we look at the blue line of Fig. 5.1 showing the public sector budget (according to the Maastricht definition), we will see a continuous improvement year by year, ending with a surplus in 2007. Indeed, Spain was used as the prime example of how a country could benefit from being a member of the Eurozone.

The red line shows the fiscal policy, which, until 2007, was nearly neutral and did not contribute to the seemingly positive development of the Spanish economy. The driving force was a real investment boom in the private sector, as being a member of the Eurozone meant a loose monetary policy. The rate of interest set by the ECB in Frankfurt was influenced by

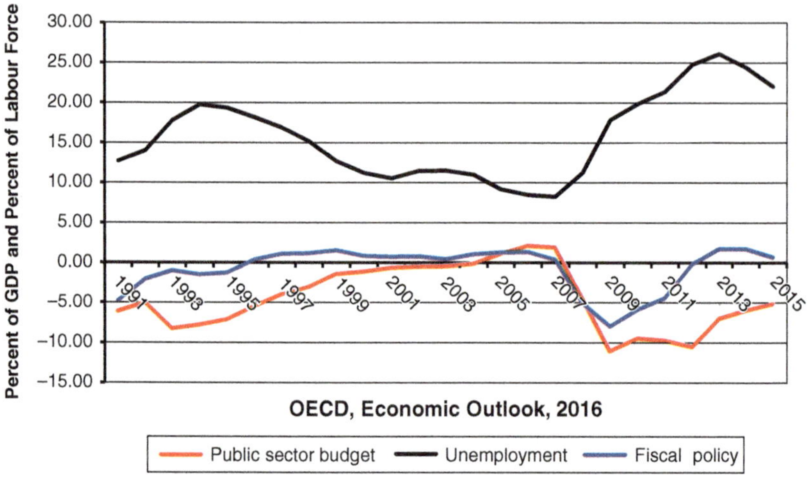

Fig. 5.2 Spain: Unemployment, public sector and fiscal policy

the low rate of inflation in Germany. Moreover, Northern European banks were more than willing to lend whatever was demanded of foreign liquidity. Due to this excess demand from the private sector, unemployment was falling and, according to the OECD calculation, even closing the output gap in 2005 where the blue line crossed the red one. Pressure in the labour market contributed to the deterioration of the Spanish international competitiveness, which had a negative impact on the balance of payments, cf. Chap. 4 (Fig. 5.2).

A closer look at the Spanish economy (see Appendix) unveils a macroeconomic causality, which is very different from the Euro-monetarist assumption of private sector equilibrium. Changes in the rate of unemployment can, to a great extent, be explained by the private sector excess savings, which may also have a significant impact at the balance of payments (current account).

The problem in the Spanish case was the squeeze between unemployment and the balance-of-payments deficit, which, at an early stage, should have been recognised by the Spanish government and, of course, the EU's institutions. The accumulating balance-of-payments deficits were unsustainable. For any realist point of view, it was obvious that Spain (like Portugal, Greece and Italy) had to improve on her international competitiveness, entailing that she needed to improve on her structural balance of payments. This proved a difficult task to accomplish, because it should not only be a matter of reducing wage costs in the tourist industries and agriculture, which would not solve the problem, anyhow. So, it is a matter of improving the structures of the more advanced sectors through a much more complicated process supported by political initiatives, where education, research, innovation and strategic public investments are integrated. The aim should be to combine these public expenditures to improve productivity and ultimately to create higher value added per working hour, which unfortunately is prevented by the requirement of a reduced public sector deficit.

Nonetheless, such a policy change from traditional production to industries of the future does not arrive by itself. It requires political leadership with focus on innovative processes, the balance of payments and employment opportunities for young people. If such a policy is successful, then the public sector budget will close by itself, given a reasonably effective tax administration. Hence, the public sector budget balance should be viewed more as a mirror of success or failure of overall economic policy, where the Euro and the restrictive budget requirements have not been helpful in any respect.

Does the Juncker Plan of 2015 Signal a (Minor) Change?

The rising unemployment and severe social crisis experienced in southern Europe have had a more direct impact on politics rather than economic arguments.

In the wake of the financial crisis in 2008, the immediate policy response of all the EU countries to the economic downturn was the provision of quite significant fiscal packages. They have concentrated on increased public investment and, where needed, the recapitalisation of private banks. For a while, these policies caused a structural deficit, adding rather large lump sum payments to the already rising public expenses incurred by the automatic stabilisers. As a consequence, the budget deficits in most countries have reached a scale never before seen in peacetime and have been considered by the monetarists to constitute a severe and unsustainable situation.

The realist argument in favour of these stimulus packages considers that, without this expansionary effect, unemployment would have continued to rise further. Looking at the development in the United States and United

Kingdom, it is undeniable that where fiscal policy has stayed on an expansionary path, there has even been a continuous fall in unemployment.

In any case, with the exception of Greece, by 2013, the rise in unemployment had come to an end in most Eurozone countries. One could almost hear the sigh of relief in the corridors of power of Brussels, Frankfurt and Berlin, when employment at last started to grow in the Eurozone as a whole. The medicine was right, it was subsequently claimed.

However, the turnaround from falling to increased employment was weak. The excess savings of the private sector were still depressingly high, making economic recovery fragile. Hence, the new EU Commission appointed in 2015 put forward real investment plans for infrastructure, renewable energies, urban renovation and sustainability activities, mainly financed by private funds. The idea is right to activate parts of the private excess savings. Furthermore, national governments have been tempted to seek exemption from the Stability Pact of funds contributed to the plan. Unfortunately, the realisation of the so-called Juncker Plan is dragging on because adequate finance is not yet available.

Public Debt Dynamics

However, unemployment will not go away by itself, especially not when the fiscal policy is rather restrictive. Although there has been some reshuffling of employment between North and South, the average unemployment rate is still above 10 percent of the active labour force and the public sector deficit is still in the aftermath of the prolonged crisis exceeding 3 percent of GDP in a number of Euro countries. Therefore, the fulfilment of the Stability Pact requires that the deficit is reduced by undertaking further public sector reductions, which had a negative impact on GDP and employment.

This negative development of reduced GDP has made it difficult to reduce the public debt/GDP ratio as long as there is a deficit in the public sector. In fact, a number a countries are caught in vicious cycle, where the current public sector deficit adds year by year to the public debt; but austerity policies make the GDP to stagnate or even to fall causing the debt ratio to go up.

Hence, in all the major Eurozone countries, except Germany, the public debt ratio has risen since 2008, independently of the rather restrictive fiscal policy which has been undertaken with the aim of balancing the public sector deficit.

Box 5.2 Debt dynamics

The mathematics of public debt dynamics is pretty simple. If the starting point is the maximum allowed by the Stability Pact of 60 percent of GDP and, say, a current deficit of 3 percent of GDP, then GDP in nominal terms has to grow by 5 percent to make the debt ratio unchanged at 60 percent.

Year 1, DEBT/GDP = 60 euro/100 euro = 0.60
Year 2, DEBT [60 + 3]/GDP [100 + 5] = 63 euro/105euro = 0.60
Year 3, DEBT [63 + 3]/GDP [105 + 5] = 66 euro/110euro = 0.60, and so on........

However, the dynamics are not as simple. When debt accumulates, it draws a tail of interest payments behind, which adds to the current deficit next year. As a rule of thumb, it is often said that a rate of interest above the growth rate in GDP (5 percent p.a. in the case above) causes interest payments to grow as a proportion of GDP.

A final, but equally important, remark concerns how public debt is financed. It is crucial to separate the public debt financed by debt instrument denominated in the country's own currency and/or by domestic savings, for example, pension funds. As we have explained in the previous chapter, a country running a balance-of-payments surplus has excess financial savings. They are often accumulated in private pension funds or banks used by government bonds issued in the domestic currency. If we examine any Eurozone country, as long as it has a surplus at the current account, then there will be excess savings which the public sector can borrow if the business cycle is weak.

As long as the private sector has a financial surplus, the public sector is not forced to pay back any debt because the private sector is accumulating a growing financial wealth. The situation is the reverse in Eurozone countries with a balance-of-payments deficit. If the government runs a current public deficit, then it has to borrow abroad and in a currency that it does not control itself, that is, in a 'foreign currency'.

Conclusion: Public Finance – Cause or Effect?

Having presented and explained the two opposing theoretical views on the role of fiscal policy, it is little wonder that the policy recommendations put forward are diverging. By fiscal policy, we mean active policies decided by government and approved by parliament with regard to the size and changes of the *underlying structural budget balance.*[2] This measure of the public balance is chosen as a condensed measure of the expansionary/contractionary effect imposed on private sector activity by government expenditures and tax revenues.

Euro-monetarists consider such an active policy as, in the best case scenario, superfluous because the private sector will adjust by itself.

Euro-realists would argue that an active fiscal policy can support the private sector and contribute to a reduced balance-of-payments deficit. In the cases where effective demand in the private sector is too small, an expansionary fiscal policy can substitute for the lack of private investment. However, the use of fiscal policy becomes double-edged if the balance of payments shows an unsustainable deficit. A contraction can be needed to reduce the deficit, but at the expense of reduce growth and increased unemployment. This dilemma is exposed in the southern European countries.

In Fig. 5.1 you can see the dilemma unfold. The fiscal policy measured by structural deficit has been rather restrictive since 2011 in most Eurozone countries. As a consequence, GDP has been falling or stagnant in those countries, which has been hardest hit by a structural budget surplus and balance-of-payments deficit. The combined impact was a steep rise in unemployment, which has activated the automatic stabilisers. We can also see that the public sector current budget has only improved a little. Hence, it is difficult to maintain the view that fiscal policy has no impact on private sector imbalances.

The Structural Budget: A Policy Goal or a Macroeconomic Instrument?

The structural budget balance is considered by Euro-monetarists to be a measure of fiscal strength. Increased surplus is a sign of 'sound' and 'responsible' fiscal policy. Conversely, a reduced surplus on the structural balance indicates that the fiscal policy has been relaxed. However, the size of a surplus cannot be taken as a measure of whether fiscal policy is *too* 'lax' or 'tight'. The structural balance is a calculation showing the balance of public budgets at 'full employment'. However, no consensus on how to define full employment or how to establish full employment is currently on offer. Furthermore, the calculation of the structural budget is very dependent on the macroeconomic model used and upon the analytical practice.

The Euro-monetarist model assumes that full employment and the balance of the structural budget coincide. As we have already discussed, 'full employment' is assumed to come by itself via the 'invisible hand'. Therefore, fiscal policy should be oriented towards balancing the structural budget. Indeed, this is the thinking behind the Financial Compact's very narrow margin for deviations of the structural budget, even during recessions! Only a deficit of a half percentage point of GDP may be accepted, no matter how high unemployment has risen.

The Euro-realists view is different. Here, the public sector is an instrument to secure better macroeconomic balance. When unemployment is high and the balance of payments is more or less under control, then the choice of an expansionary fiscal policy to counterweigh excess savings in the private sector is a relevant policy option. It might increase both the structural deficit and the current deficit. In any case, it could be the right policy to initiate a process of falling unemployment and growing GDP, which could kick-start a recovery and cause the public debt ratio to fall.

How Do Governments Avoid Public Debt Ratios to go on Growing?

Once again the two views differ.

The Euro-monetarists only look at the public sector. If the budget shows a deficit, then public debt is growing, although it is necessarily measured as a percent of GDP. It is the debt–GDP ratio which matters. Here, the development in the GDP is at least as important as the budget deficit. Just after the Second World War, the British debt–GDP ratio was around 200 percent, but by the end of the 1960s, the debt ratio had been reduced to less than 40 percent mainly due to growth in nominal GDP.

However, a falling or stagnant GDP, combined with a substantial current public sector deficit, is a venomous cocktail. In this case, the public debt ratio is growing despite attempts to undertake a restrictive fiscal policy. If growth does not resume within a short period, then the public finances measured by the debt ratio is not sustainable. In that case, the automatic stabilisers have to be reduced together and the other current public expenditures and tax rates increased. A vicious spiral will then be set in motion.

The Euro-realists start looking at the private sector and the balance of payments and then asking themselves: where should we find the cause of excess private savings? If the balance of payments shows a (substantial) deficit – an improvement has to be undertaken by increased competitiveness. However, those countries with a structural balance-of-payments surplus should be committed to undertaking an expansionary fiscal policy as long as unemployment is above any reasonable definition of 'full employment'. This expansionary policy could go hand in hand with a controlled deterioration of the international competitive position or foreign direct investments in Eurozone countries with a structural balance-of-payments deficit. This latter initiative could be organised through the European Investment bank providing funds for the Juncker Plan.

In the end, the best medicine to avoid a continuous growth in public debt is a prosperous private sector and a reduced rate unemployment and external balance, so,

> Look after Unemployment, and the Budget will look after itself
>
> Keynes 1933

Appendix Spain: Getting Causality Right!

To add some further empirical support to my arguments related to 'Macroeconomic imbalances: cause and effect', I have calculated correlations for the main relations.[3]

Of course, I know that statistical significance is not a proof of causality, but it may constitute support for realist arguments put forward in the theoretical sections of the chapter.

In Fig. A1, we see a relationship where the level of private sector excess savings causes unemployment. In fact, an increase of 1 percent point of

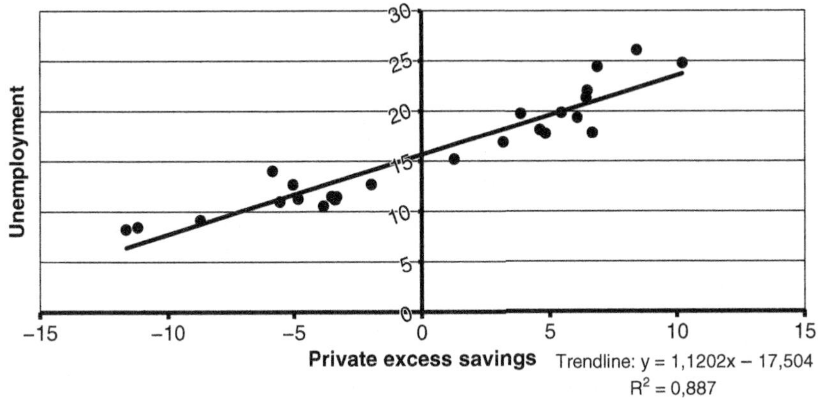

Fig. A1 Spain: Private excess savings versus unemployment
Source: OECD, Economic Outlook, 2016

excess savings has made unemployment go up by 0.71 points in the historical period examined here. The significance of this result is pretty high with an R^2 of 0.91.

There is also a significant relationship between private excess savings and the balance of payments. When savings rise, less goods and services are imported and the current account is improved. This is the most likely explanation looking at Spain because if the positive correlation had been caused by increased export then it would have had a reducing impact on employment, which was not the case cf. Figs. A1 and A2.

Now we have established a causality chain in the Spanish case from excess private savings via unemployment and rather strong automatic budget stabilisers to public finances. As can be seen in Fig. A3, an increase in unemployment make the public sector budget deteriorate by 0.81 percent point (measured as proportion of GDP). The statistical correlation is quite significant with an R^2 of 0.81.

Hence, no wonder that the Spanish public sector budget improved during the booming period of 1998–2007, which unfortunately made to government relax and the EU Commission give the wrong recommendation.

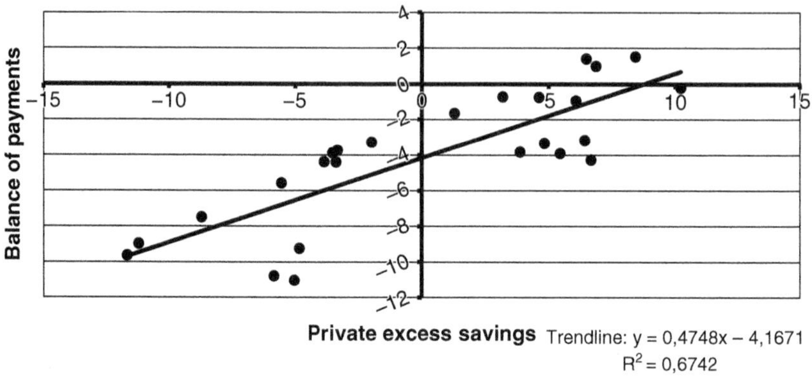

Fig. A2 Spain: Private excess savings – balance of payments
Source: OECD, Economic Outlook, 2016

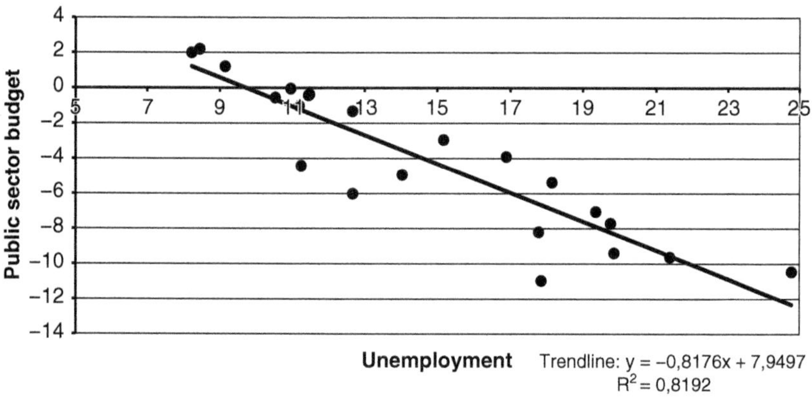

Fig. A3 Spain: Unemployment and public sector budget
Source: OECD, Economic Outlook, 2016

The missed opportunities to restructure the Spanish economy is a disgrace for which Spain and the EU institution may share the responsibility. However, in view of the institutional set-up framing the Eurozone members, there are few opportunities to overcome this missed opportunity.

Notes

1. The underestimation of the output gap might also explain why United Kingdom, according to this calculation, has a rather expansionary fiscal policy.
2. I have chosen to use the underlying primary budget in a number of cases, therefore avoiding that only a single instance of public income or expenditures, automatic stabilisers and interest payments disturb the overall picture of the size and direction of discretionary fiscal policy.
3. There was a significant shift in Spanish fiscal policy as a consequence of the Euro crisis, causing a break in the time series and the underlying policy structures, which according to the Lucas critique lends support to the view that the time series analysis should be concentrated on a homogeneous period.

CHAPTER 6

Macroeconomic Imbalances: Unemployment and Inequality

Abstract The macroeconomic development in the Eurozone (as a whole) and the major non-Euro countries has been significantly different since 2010. Unemployment in the Eurozone is still much higher than previously, but very unequally distributed. The Euro-realist explanation is lack of effective demand and huge balance-of-payments imbalances within the Eurozone. The Euro-monetarist have to the contrary recommended fiscal restrain and internal devaluations in deficit countries causing stagnating output, increased inequality and a falling wage rate, which tends to 'beggar yourself and your neighbours' by a kind of 'race to bottom'.

The non-Euro countries have fared somewhat better by taking stock on their monetary sovereignty through currency devaluations and more relaxed monetary and fiscal policies.

Keywords Misunderstood fiscal austerity · Internal devaluation · Beggar-thou-neighbour wage policy · Increased inequality · Race to the bottom · Unprecedented unemployed

Introduction

The previous chapters have explained why macroeconomists are divided on economic policies. They have two fundamentally different visions of the macroeconomic system which spill over into their views on the economic consequences of the Euro.

J. Jespersen, *The Euro*, DOI 10.1007/978-3-319-46388-9_6

From a human perspective, as well as the real sectors of the economy, unemployment is the largest scourge. On the individual level, involuntary unemployment is a personal humiliation, while at the macro level it is a waste of resources.

Views differ on the causes of unemployment, but it cannot be denied that unemployment at the European economy as a whole has been persistently high since the 1980s (see Fig. 6.1). In addition, one can see that since the outbreak of the economic crisis of 2008, as an average of the participating countries, unemployment has been taken been higher inside than outside of the Eurozone.

The monetarists claim that if there are no impediments to the working of the 'invisible hand' and a well-organised market economic system, then the best policy is to have no policy at all. Any discussion of the 'optimum currency area' is only about the size and the difficulties of overcoming these obstacles. Calculation of these transactions costs is considered principally as both an empirical and a political task to overcome or at least reduce the obstacles to the working of 'free' market forces.

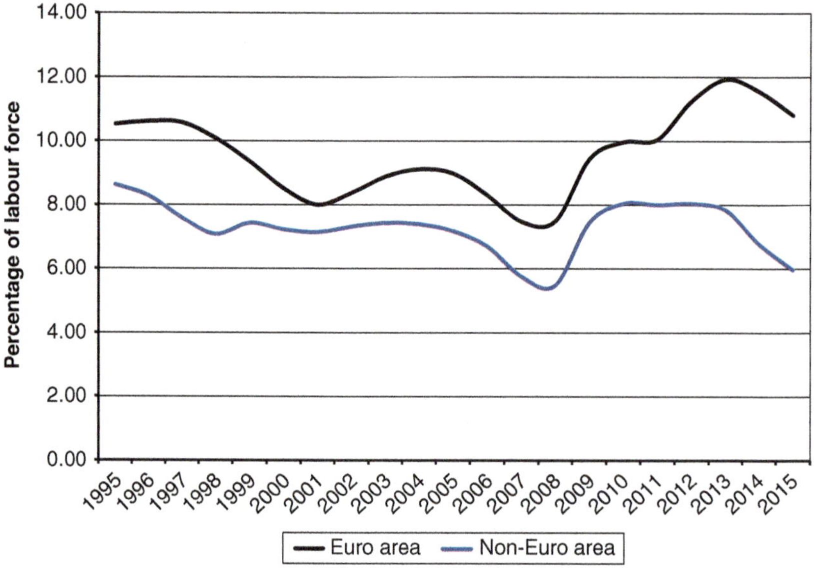

Fig. 6.1 Unemployment Eurozone and non-Eurozone

For instance, when Milton Friedman warned against the EMU in the 1990s, his main argument was that a premature common currency in Europe would increase European inflexibility, or so-called Euro-sclerosis. Moreover, in his opinion, labour market reforms and increased trans-border trade would reduce transaction costs and inflexibility little by little, so reducing the relevancy of keeping the exchange rate flexible.

Hence, according to monetarist theory, macroeconomic imbalances have been caused either by weak market structures or by misguided policy. The best cure to these ills is a combination of structural reforms, balanced budgets and 'patience' necessary to ensure the support of the Euro in the longer run. The aspiration was that the macroeconomic imbalances observed would then disappear by themselves, although taking some time. In this meantime of adjustment, national politicians should learn to cope with macroeconomic misalignments like unemployment without taking expansionary initiatives. The founding fathers of the EMU had their suspicions that politicians would be 'soft' and therefore wanted to box in fiscal policy by a number of restrictions specified in the EU Treaty. When the plan for a common currency was launched, the president of the German Bundesbank, Carl Otto Pöhl, see Delors-report (1989), was not convinced that the participating countries would respect the rules of the game. According to this view, right from the very beginning of the EMU, the EU Treaty should have specified a roadmap for establishing a political union guaranteeing the overall coordination of national budgets and some kind of an automatic transfer mechanism among member countries. Instead, the implementation of this federalist plan had to wait until the Euro crisis had revealed the fragility of the present EMU construction. Hence, the room for disagreements remained substantial and the popular resistance towards further federalism within the EU was given momentum to grow.

The realist view on macroeconomics is fundamentally different. Here, the macroeconomic system in one country is not considered as self-adjusting. A macroeconomic system containing more nations with a different history, structures and political preferences will therefore be even less self-adjusting. For realists, this is not a matter of fixed or flexible exchange rates, nor is it a guarantee of stability. The main support of the realist claim is the nature of the historical development of Europe.

For the past 40 years, European unemployment has been above a level, which, by any reasonable argument, can be considered as 'full employment'.

When most unemployed people are asked 'Would you like a job?' the answer is 'Yes, of course.' Furthermore, there are no realistic theory which can argue in favour of private financial savings and real investment being of equal size at the level of full employment.

The observations and conclusions of realists are an echo of Maynard Keynes's contributions to macroeconomics. He was also the intellectual father of the international monetary system established just after the war. In the final chapter of this book, we will discuss how a similar but modernised financial system could be organised within Europe as a part of a wider international monetary system.

We have already studied two important macroeconomic imbalances: the balance-of-payments surplus and deficits and private savings/investment discrepancy. We have noted that they are both sub-imbalances within the macroeconomic system as a whole; not only at the national level but with a number of spillover effects from one country to the other via the balance of payments (current and capital accounts). In this chapter, we shall mainly look at unemployment from a realist perspective, in recognition that unemployment does not go away by itself.[1]

Causes of Unemployment

> The outstanding faults of the economic society in which we live are its failure to provide for full employment and its arbitrary and inequitable distribution of wealth and income. (Keynes 1936, p. 372)

Unemployment means a waste of real resources and a social scourge, which are two good reasons to get rid of unemployment and accordingly to improve the common good. But the private sector cannot adjust by itself to full employment. It needs a helping hand from the government. According to realist theory, 'effective demand' is a necessary condition to guide the economic development. Unfortunately, this guiding hand has been weakened by the reduction of and restriction on the use of national policy instruments.

1. The arguments why effective demand is so important have already been put forward in Chap. 2 and will be repeated here. Firms' decision on production is the driving force in a capitalist market economy, so when firms find it profitable to produce more goods and services, that is, a positive profit margin, they have an incentive.

2. But it is of crucial importance that firms also have expectations to be able to sell the increased output, that is, that demand will pick up in the (near) future.
3. Then firms increase production and demand more labour.

One could formulate these conditions very briefly; namely, in a market economy where prices are given, unit costs are decisive but, without reasonably firm expectations that people will buy the output, it is not profitable to produce, however. The fulfilment of these two requirements is Keynes's theoretical breakthrough in *The General Theory*. Hence, *effective demand* is a combination of supply consideration (profitability) and demand consideration (expectations).

This conclusion with regard to effective demand holds in a closed as well as an open economy. For the single, smaller firms, the market price is given, roughly speaking, which is often the case for standardised goods, such as agricultural, textiles and simple manufacturing products, especially at the European market. If price competition is rather strong, the development in unit (labour) cost measured in a common currency becomes very important for profitability and is often referred to as *international competitiveness.*

Profitability: The Margin Between Market Price and Unit (Labour) Cost

Small open economies have the option of improving the profit margin by implementing a different kind of wage policy, serving to strengthen the incentive to sell more goods (and services) abroad. On the other hand, such wage-reducing policies have partly a negative impact on domestic consumption because they reduce the disposable income of wage earners and so increase the real value of debt. This rising level of debt then has to be counter-balanced by increased value of financial assets. Such wage/cost policies are usually called an *internal devaluation*.

However, it should be acknowledged that increased exports (even if from a small country) will be expressed in terms of an increased level of imports having a depressing effect on the importing economy. International trade is a zero-sum accounting principle: to export from one country is to import on the part of another. In this way, exporting countries gain jobs and income, while importing countries lose jobs and income. It is only in cases where international trade has a positive derived effect that the sum of trade becomes positive, although still unevenly distributed.

In larger countries where foreign trade constitutes a smaller share of GDP, the negative domestic effect of an internal devaluation might dominate the positive export effect. Moreover, in cases where a number of countries undertake wage-reducing policies at the very same time, this will result in a mutual and self-enforcing negative effect, where reduced consumption in one country reduces imports from abroad, meaning less exports and reduced output for both the trading partners. This might trigger a negative chain effect quite similar to the 'Beggar thy neighbour' policy, which was the outcome of a sequence of devaluations (and import control) in the 1930s.

Effective Domestic and Foreign Demand

As mentioned earlier, *effective demand* consists of two elements: profitability (supply considerations) and expected demand (sales considerations).

For obvious reasons, 'expected demand' cannot be measured precisely because it is a psychological phenomenon influenced by some objective factors, such as purchasing power and credit availability, both domestic and abroad, in combination with optimism and pessimism.

As Keynes wrote, it would be pure chance if effective demand should coincide with output at full employment. In reality, the financial savings of the private sector are not coordinated with real investment plans. As we have quite frequently seen, there may be an excess of savings causing unemployment. If we assume that the profit margin is acceptable, then economic policy could boost aggregate demand. This explains why giving up demand management policies *de*stabilises macroeconomic development and makes it difficult, if not impossible to reduce unemployment, especially in the Eurozone.

According to the principles of the EU Treaty, monetary policy within the Eurozone is organised in accordance with monetarist theory; that is, with a focus on controlling consumer price inflation where hardly any consideration is given to the performance of the real economy. It is only quite recently that monetary policy has shifted and price development has approached being part of a deflationary process. However, as we see in the next chapter, this policy has had little success.

In the previous chapter, we explained why excess private savings could cause unemployment to rise, thereby activating automatic budget stabilisers and partly, but only partly compensating for the reduced demand. In recessions, a counter-cyclical fiscal policy is needed to fully compensate the increased imbalance within the private sector. In practice, this means that a discretionary fiscal policy could reduce the real sector imbalance, which is calculated as an increased structural deficit. Accordingly, a fixed (and narrow) limit on the accepted structural public sector budget would block the use of fiscal policy as a counter-cyclical measure.

Thus, in a situation with substantial unemployment, it is difficult to argue against an expansionary fiscal policy, especially in countries with a balance-of-payments surplus. In fact, one could argue the reverse more easily, that a surplus country should reduce unemployment at home by increasing domestic demand and production. Furthermore, such an expansionary policy would spill over as increased imports from other EU countries, which would be a relief.

In Fig. 6.2 we see the important difference between the fiscal policy in the Eurozone as a whole and the main non-Eurozone countries. Here, fiscal policy is measured by a 'structural primary budget'. Although unemployment in the Eurozone was at its highest point ever, fiscal policy became contractive in 2011. It is no wonder that unemployment has continued to stay high.

The development in the non-Eurozone countries has been different for a number of reasons. One explanatory difference was the presence of an expansionary fiscal policy, although this effect was reduced after 2010.

A 'Race to the Bottom' in the Eurozone?

After 2008, the positive economic development experienced by non-Euro countries (and Germany) was supported by improved international competitiveness obtained partly through currency devaluations. As we argued in Chap. 4, these currency depreciations were not applauded by the trading partners, as development in international competitiveness is a zero-sum game. The world as a whole clearly cannot improve its 'international' competitiveness, but countries keeping their own currency have more freedom to improve their competitive position by unilateral devaluations.

This currency devaluation came as a market response to, when the monetary policy were made more expansive, which was the case in the United States and the United Kingdom at an early stage shortly after 2009. The Eurozone was initially the loser in this game, while undertaking a more restrictive monetary policy, see Chap. 7. However, the impact for the Eurozone as a whole would not be that significant because the largest

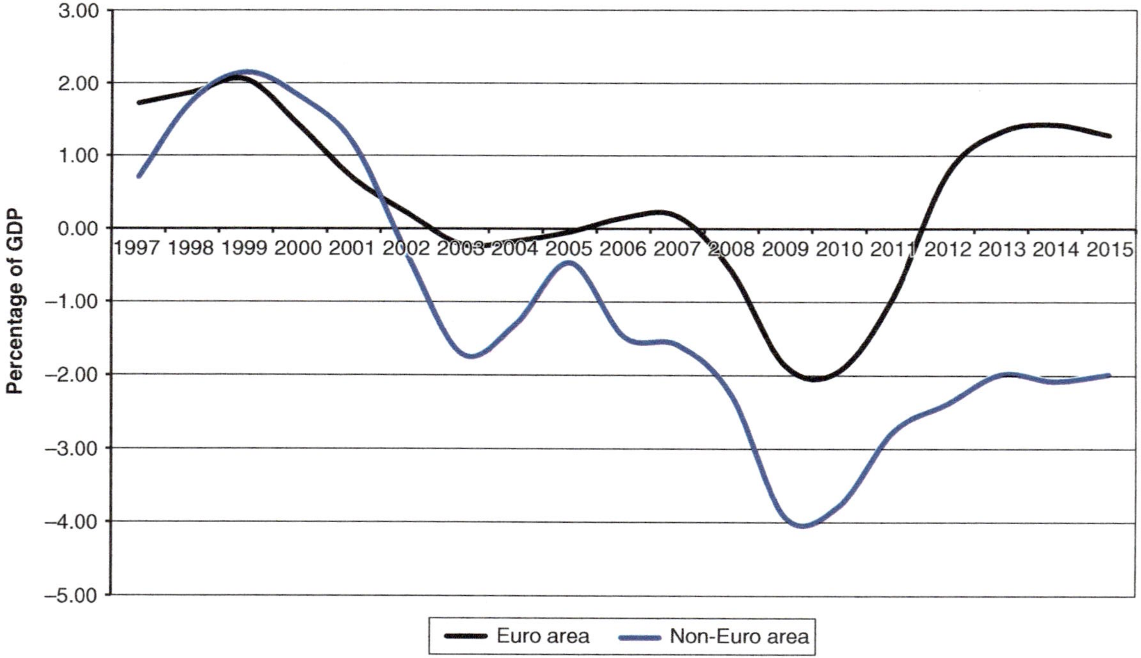

Fig. 6.2 Fiscal policy in Eurozone and non-Euro countries

Note: The value of zero signals a 'neutral' fiscal policy. A positive number indicates contraction; but when unemployment is high an expansionary policy is needed to stabilise the private sector production

Source: OECD, Economic Outlook, 2016

share of Eurozone foreign trade is by other Euro members, where exchange rate de- and re-valuations are, by definition, ruled out, unless a Eurozone country decides to leave the EMU.

Improvements in one country's competitive position within the Eurozone occur as a consequence of the relative development in unit (labour) cost, that is, the hourly wages corrected for productivity gains. If one country gains, at least one other country has to lose. It is consequently a relationship between the domestic development in cost and the development in cost abroad. One country can only improve her competitive position if she is doing better than the average of her trading partners. As long as competition is strong and the market price is determined by the average marginal cost within the entire intra-EU market trade becomes a zero-sum game. One country's exports are other country's imports. Through this market process, jobs are gained in one country and lost at an equal amount in the importing countries. This happens either directly when, for instance, German cars are preferred to Spanish cars or indirectly, when domestic purchasing power is used on buying foreign goods or services (tourism) instead of domestically produced goods and services.

Accordingly, within the Eurozone, countries can only improve their export on the expenses of the trading partner by reducing unit (labour) cost below the average of the Eurozone as a whole. So, the political ambition of reducing unit labour cost could easily develop into a 'race to the bottom', where competing wage reduction becomes the norm with negative consequences for effective demand; that is, weak private consumption and real debt increase.

What could be described as a kind of a race towards the bottom can be seen in Fig. 6.3 from 2008. In the southern European countries the unit labour cost index has fallen, but is still above the euro average and way above the German, although both parties have gained from the falling dollar/euro exchange rate since 2014, see Fig. 7.1. The consequence is that the Eurozone is gaining and increasing its net export; but, of course, at the expense of its trading partners outside the Eurozone. This improvement is partly due to a reduced exchange rate and to falling unit labour cost.

Accordingly, the Eurozone has improved its international competitive position in the world market. However, it should be noted that, at the global level, competitiveness is a relative concept. The world market

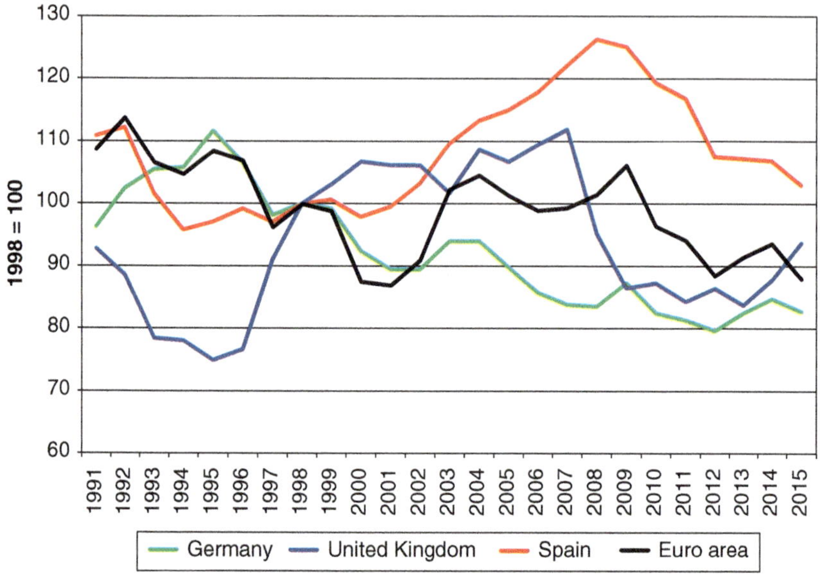

Fig. 6.3 International competitiveness, Euro countries

Source: OECD, Economic Outlook, 2016

depends on how unit cost changes in the United States, China, the non-Eurozone countries and for other trading partners. In addition, the euro exchange rates do play an important role. Once again we are dealing with a relative concept. The development of the exchange rate depends on economic factors in both the Eurozone and the United States, or any other country with a floating exchange rate policy.

As we saw in Fig. 4.1, there has been a rather significant increase in the surplus of the Eurozone's overall balance of payments. However, it is difficult to conclude whether this changed situation has been caused by the major drop in the euro exchange rate improving international competitiveness or much weaker growth of GDP in the Eurozone compared with major trading partners.

In any case, the surplus at the Eurozone current account is counterbalanced by financial capital exports of equal and substantial size. This capital export is partly explained by the relatively expansionary monetary policy that was undertaken by the ECB from 2013 onwards, discussed in Chap. 7.

Social Consequences of the Euro and the 'Race to the Bottom'[2]

'The race to the bottom' has social consequences. There has been a persistent call from EU institutions that member countries and especially members of the EMU make their labour markets more flexible with regard to wages, labour market regulation and reduced welfare spending. This call is an echo of the monetarist way of thinking.

Germany took the lead in the Eurozone in the early 2000s under initiative and informal leadership of the chancellor Gerhard Schröder and his social democratic government. The outcome was the so-called Hartz laws whose main purpose was to roll back the welfare state, create incentives for workers to take up low-wage jobs and so establish a downward pressure on wages. For more than 10 years (1998–2008), Germany's unit labour cost was nearly unchanged. Meanwhile, the unemployment rate was one of the highest amongst the EMU countries. Little by little though, German exports gained momentum at the expense of the southern European countries derailed by a construction boom due to the low rate of interest within the Eurozone (Table 6.1).

Nonetheless, it is striking that the number of people at risk of poverty and social exclusion within the Eurozone has gone up since 2005, even though the years 2005–2008 were prosperous with a falling rate of unemployment. Germany's shrinking of her welfare state showed itself in the statistics, of poverty, social exclusion and distribution. Her main trading partners within

Table 6.1 People at risk of poverty or social exclusion

				2005–2008	*2005–2014*	*2008–2014*
1000 persons	**2005**	**2008**	**2014**	Change	Change	Change
EU(27)	124.339	116.584	121.085	−7.755	−3.254	4.501
Non-Euro	**56.094**	**46.682**	**44.703**	**−9.412**	**−11.391**	**−1.979**
Euro (17)	**68.245**	**69.902**	**76.382**	**1.657**	**8.137**	**6.480**
Germany	15.022	16.345	16.508	1.323	1.486	163
Greece	3.131	3.046	3.885	−85	754	839
Spain	10.481	11.124	13.402	643	2.921	2.278
France	11.127	11.150	11.540	23	413	390
Italy	14.621	15.099	17.146	478	2.525	2.047
United Kingdom	14.530	14.069	15.188	−461	658	1.119

Source: Eurostat

Table 6.2 Gini coefficients

	2001	*2008*	*2014*	*2001–2014*
Germany	25	30.2	30.7	+5.7
Spain	33	32.4	34.7	+1.7
Italy	29	31.2	32.4	+3.3
France	27	29.8	29.2	+2.2
United Kingdom	35	33.9	31.6	–3.4

Source: Eurostat (http://ec.europa.eu/eurostat/tgm/table.do?tab=table&init=1&language=en&pcode=tessi190&plugin=1)

the Eurozone were recommended by Brussels and the Euro-monetarists to follow suit. This should be seen in contrast to 'non-Euro countries'. This entry shows a significantly different picture mainly because the eastern European countries have managed deliberately to transform economic growth into poverty reduction through this period, by creating jobs and seeking to improve minimum social standards. Furthermore, it should be noted that the United Kingdom demonstrated its independence in economic policy by reducing poverty in the period 2005–2008; but turned around after the financial crisis had hit and the government had changed.

We might now turn our attention to a broader concept of inequality measured by the Gini coefficient (Table 6.2).[3]

In many ways, it is not surprising that inequality has risen in tandem with a growing number of people in poverty and a shrunken welfare state.

However, according to realist theory, rising inequality increases the risk of macroeconomic stagnation. Once again, we can gain an insight into these trends by turning our attention to the concluding chapter of Keynes's *General Theory*. Here, Keynes's concern is mainly with the capacity of inequality to reduce effective demand, being that poor people have a higher propensity to spend, while the rich are more likely to save. Therefore, for a while, during the 2000s, poor people borrowed (from banks) to keep up their consumption thereby creating a debt overload, when banks then ran into difficulties and stopped over night its loose lending procedures, this contributed to the burst of the credit bubble.

During the crisis, we saw that excess savings increase in the private sector, because the rich people and those who still had a job were saving, while the poor and those who lost their job had little purchasing power to spend. A situation which was further aggregated by cuts in the welfare state and other public expenses due to the requirements of the Stability

Pact (and later also the Fiscal Compact). Hence, the public sector was prevented to give a helping hand converting passive private savings into active public investments. When unemployment rose and the size of welfare states were reduced, inequality continued to rise. In short, a vicious circle had been initiated, where cuts in one country spread to other countries via the trade balance, which would further reinforce the race to the bottom.

Conclusion: Macroeconomic Imbalances Have Increased

According to the realist analysis, it is a necessary condition that, to make the EMU sustainable, participating countries do not deviate too much from one another.

This reality is particularly important to consider in view of the fact that there is no mutual commitment to support those countries running into difficulties. Equally important is that fact that no 'punishment' is imposed on countries that take advantage of the common currency by applying 'beggar-thou-neighbour' policy.

In Fig. 6.4 we have presented an index showing macroeconomic imbalance in four larger European countries plus the Eurozone as a whole. The index is just the sum of the rate of unemployment and the balance-of-payments deficit (per cent of GDP). In addition to a unit (labour) cost index, this index could have been used in as one of the convergence criteria back in the 1998, when selection of the member state of the EMU took place.

It is obvious that Spain was divergent from the very beginning. However, Germany, France, Italy and the United Kingdom had a relatively similar macroeconomic situation. Until 2005, all of these countries had a rather similar development, although the United Kingdom had a flexible exchange rate. On the other hand, Germany started to improve her balance of payments, but, in the beginning, at the expense of higher unemployment. It was not until 2006 that Germany showed up in the statistics as the diverging country, causing tension within the EMU. If we had added an index for unit labour cost, then it would have unveiled the underlying emerging imbalance at an early stage. In any case, having set up the EMU construction without any commitment to preventing surplus countries from taking advantage of the other members via the balance of payments, nothing could have stopped Germany. German officials repeatedly defended

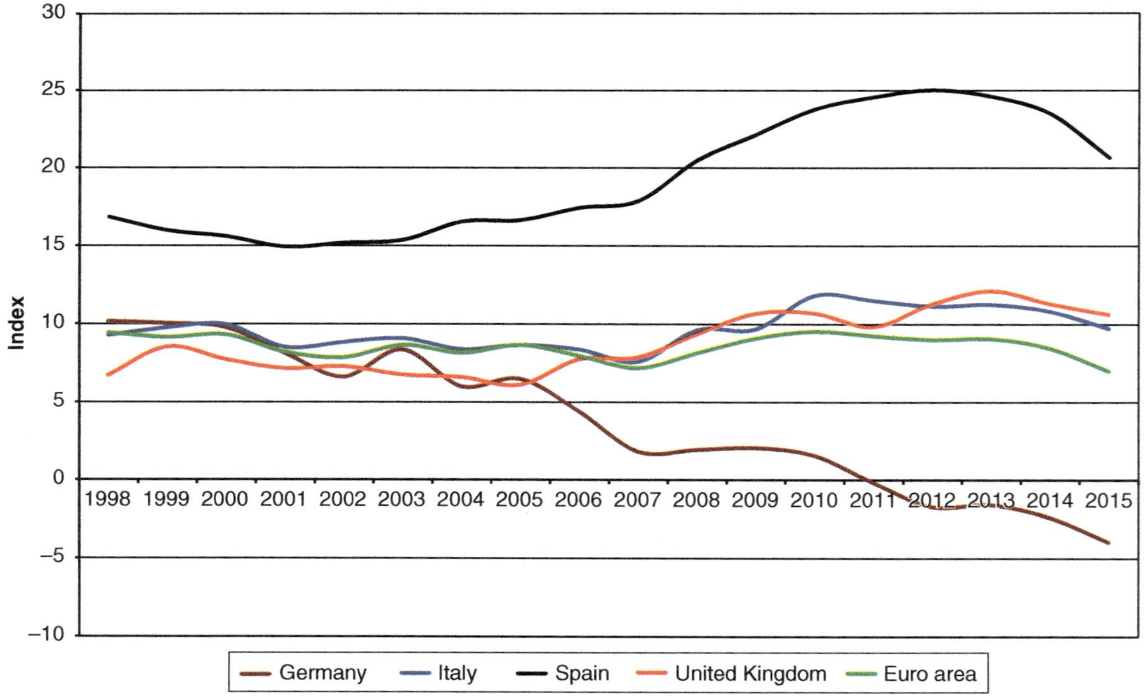

Fig. 6.4 Macroeconomic imbalances in the major EU countries

Note: Macroeconomic imbalance is defined as the sum of unemployment and balance of payments deficit

Source: OECD, Economic Outlook, 2016 and own calculation

themselves by saying that other countries could just have done the same. The point is that within a zero-game system, all the participants could not improve on competitiveness!

This development has demonstrated that the EMU institutional framework is missing an automatic creditor brake as a mechanism that could stop one (or more) country/ies going on accumulating financial wealth at the expense of other members. Debt accumulation could go on only as long as the banks of the creditor member state(s) were willing to supply loans (and liquidity) to the banks/firms in the deficit countries. The process of financial re-circulation from surplus to deficit countries was argued by the Euro supporters to be risk-free; it was therefore of no concern as long as loan transactions took place in the same currency. However, they were wrong because the accumulating country risks could deviate and, in the end, they did deviate substantially. As we shall see in next chapter, the banks of the creditor country suddenly realised that they had made far too many loans to the financially more insecure banks in the deviant deficit countries.

In 2008, the financial system fell apart, triggering multiple financial crises that spilled over into an international banking crisis. The financial system in north and south Europe needed governmental support, which became extremely costly.

This story of how public finances eventually came under severe pressure has been covered in the previous chapter.

For the time being, the Eurozone countries have been given a breathing space thanks to the surplus (or near surplus) at the balance of payments of all the EMU countries except Greece. However, this will only last until the surrounding world (United States, United Kingdom and the oil-exporting countries) decides to stop running a balance-of-payments deficit.

Hence, a global trade (and exchange rate) war is looming and could easily trigger a new Euro crisis.

Notes

1. Within the history of economic thought, it is the opposing view that 'supply of labour creates its own demand' which is eternally long and repeated with monetarist and new classical theory. I will not go into it again here because it does not correspond with the present-day reality.

2. I can strongly recommend the book on *Social Europe: A Dead End; What the Eurozone Crisis is doing to Europe's Social Dimension*, edited by Arnaud Lechevalier and Jan Wilgohs, Copenhagen, Djøf Publishing
3. Broadly speaking, the Gini-coefficient measures a hypothetical calculation of the share of disposable income, which has to be transferred from people above the median income to people below the median income to make the distribution equal, i.e. a Gini coefficient of zero.

CHAPTER 7

Distressed European Central Bank and Financial Instability

Abstract Following the recommendation by Euro-monetarists, the European Central Bank's major responsibility is to secure price stability in the Eurozone by inflation targeting. In reality, the European Central Bank (ECB) had little impact on developments in money supply (M3) and price inflation. Banks behaviour, financial markets and the euro exchange rate were dominated by market forces, which led to financial stress. When the financial crisis hit in 2008/2009 countries with balance-of-payments deficits and large foreign debt had increasing difficulties to get access to capital markets. First, EU set up rescue funds providing emergency loans, later the ECB started to act as lender of last resort. In both cases, debtor countries had to accept strict conditionalities, which prolonged the stagnation within the Eurozone as a whole.

Keywords European Central Bank · Misguided monetary policy · Inflation targeting · Monetary instability · Dis-integrated capital markets · Lender of last resort

Introduction: Two Views on Money and Finance

Once again, we have to clear up the two fundamentally different positions to which we have referred in regard to European macroeconomics. Now we have become familiar with the Euro-monetarist way of thinking, it will be relatively simple to present the view on money and finance and the arguments behind the independence of the European Central Bank

J. Jespersen, *The Euro*, DOI 10.1007/978-3-319-46388-9_7

(ECB). As usual, it is more difficult to give a short presentation of the Euro-realist view on money and finance because it is here that the economy as a whole is placed in focus.

a. **The Euro-monetarist view on macroeconomics** is to argue that 'money is a veil' with no impact on the real economy in the medium-/long-term perspectives. As we have mentioned repeatedly, the argument here is that the private sector of the market economic system are considered as self-adjusting. Hence, full employment (the level of natural unemployment) and a closed output gap come by itself. Any political interference will impede this smooth adjustment process. The financial sector acts only as a facilitator reducing transaction costs, when savings seek real investments and vice versa. The flexible rate of interest ensures that all savings are invested in real and produced capital goods.

   Money is only a means of exchange, one reducing barter cost. Hence, the conclusion reached is that the only lasting impact of monetary policy is upon the consumer price level. The above is considered as a purely technical relationship, known as the *quantity theory of money and prices*. Therefore, it is recommended that control of the money supply be left to a politically independent Board of ECB Directors. Hence, measures should be taken to ensure that politicians do not abuse the power of the printing press for short-term political interference to obtain populist gains shortly before an election is called. In addition, the imposition of restrictions has been recommended to reduce the activities of banks and other financial institutions. Here, the argument revolves around the question of, who is expected to know the risk of lending the best? The answer: those who undertake the lending. Furthermore, as Friedman has argued, speculation is a good thing because if it is correct, it speeds up the adjustment, while if it is wrong, speculators lose money and are driven out of the market, leaving only the good ones there.
b. **The Euro-monetarists' international view** is similar. Who is to know that international lending and borrowing the best? Answer: those banks and other financial institutions who undertake these activities. Furthermore, a balance of payments deficit/surplus does not constitute a macroeconomic problem as long as they are rooted in the optimising behaviour of private individual. A balance-of-payments deficit in country A is, as we know, a balance-of-payments

surplus in another country B. Thus, investment opportunities in country A are considered in both countries as superior to investments in country B. It is therefore argued that rational actors in country B invest their savings in country A, so closing the balance of payments deficit automatically! Hence, the Euro-monetarists argue that they do not see any problem with, for instance, the German balance of payments surplus. In fact, quite the opposite is the case, as it is used to finance real investments in the deficit countries. They should rather be grateful. This argument may sound convincing in a two-people-two-goods world with full information, but reality tells another story – ask the Greeks, the Spaniards, the Portuguese, etc. Although Spain had a balanced public sector budget leading up to the financial crash, the automatic recycling of the Spanish current account deficit stopped all at once in 2008 and a much higher rate of interest was required by 'the markets'.

Hence, we will now turn our attention to what has happened in reality and search for a plausible explanation.

c. In the **Euro-realists' domestic view,** 'money and the real world'[1] cannot be separated. It is completely out of touch with reality to assume that 'money is only a veil'. Money, finance and any real economic activity cannot be separated for two obvious reasons. The first one is the simple fact that any economic transaction involves money because 'money buys goods, goods buy money; but goods do not buy goods' to quote Clower (1965). The other equally weighty argument is that the real economy is not in equilibrium under any relevant understanding of this concept.

   We only need to look at unemployment and how it has evolved through the past 40 years. Here, money, banking and finance and the institutional settings are crucial to understanding macroeconomic development. We have to put forward separate arguments concerning the interrelationship between the financial and the real sectors at the domestic and at the intra-monetary union level, being that private banks and financial institutions are regulated at the national level.

   It is a requirement of the EU Treaty that the central bank in any member country becomes independent of the political decision process. The government may define the range of price inflation for the central bank to aim at, but the use of monetary policy instruments is at the sole discretion of the central bank. With regard to the ECB, the Treaty is even more specific with regard to independence. Here, it is the board of directors who define 'price stability' and how to obtain it; if they fail, then it has no direct consequences for the governors!

According to realist theory, by accepting the task, the central bank undertakes an impossible job of controlling price inflation uniquely by monetary instruments: that is, the interest rate and supply of central bank money. Here we should take into account that consumer price development is an outcome of the interaction between demand and supply within the real part of the economy and so monetary instruments are of little use. Notably, during periods with excess supply capacity – that is, unemployment – it is largely unit labour cost which dominates the market price for goods and services (see Chap. 6 on effective demand). Unit labour cost is determined partly by money wage and partly by productivity. Both variables are, to a large extent, determined by endogenous factors within the economic system as a whole.

In addition, structures in the labour market and technological innovations play a role, which is often presented as a kind of an elaborated Phillips Curve for each country (see Forder (2014) for a critical discussion of the (lack of) theoretical foundation of the Phillips Curve). If this realist approach is accepted, then it becomes obvious that monetary policy instruments have no direct impact and hardly any indirect effect on consumer prices, except possibly setting a kind of expectation framework around the wage-bargaining process.

d. **Euro-realist international view on money and finance** Monetary policy, that is, the rate of interest and supply of liquidity, does have an impact on external transaction via the balance of payments, especially on the capital account, and for most countries outside the EMU in terms of the foreign exchange rate. As discussed in Chap. 4, a deficit in the current account has to be compensated by a surplus in the capital account to avoid a loss of international liquidity.

   If the country under consideration has a floating exchange rate, then it will adjust in the foreign exchange market until a financial capital inflow (a surplus at the capital account) equalises the overall balance of payments. Here, the central bank has a role to play. Under normal conditions, the foreign capital account is rather sensitive to even minor changes in the international differential of short-term interest rates. Nonetheless, the central bank might take a critical view of a falling exchange rate because it causes import prices to rise and have an impact on the domestic unit cost level and therefore upon consumer price inflation.

In reality, very few countries with their own currency have committed themselves to a fixed exchange rate policy. It makes the foreign adjustment process rather rigid, as monetary policy is fixed to the defence of the exchange rate. Usually, it is only countries with a comfortable surplus at the current account, which, for political reasons, might follow a fixed exchange rate policy; this is the case, for instance, with Denmark at the cost of more financial instability such as asset and house price bubbles and bank insolvencies.

Balance of Payments, Capital Account

A deficit on the current account of the balance of payments has to be financed by external financial resources. This is where the capital account of the balance of payments comes into the argument. The deficit has to be counter-weighed by a surplus on the capital account. It means that international money has to be borrowed abroad, unless the deficit country possesses foreign reserves.

This monetary relationship relates to a country with its own national currency, which is only accepted as a means of payments domestically, like for instance the non-Euro countries.

Today, without any international capital control, transaction on the capital account consists of financial flows directed by the relative rates of interest. A surplus can be established by raising the rate of interest. This procedure goes quite well as long as the creditworthiness and solvency of the financial institutions of the borrowing country is not questioned. These international capital flows ensure that the current and capital accounts quite easily equalise as long as the foreign debt is within a reasonable size compared to GDP. Furthermore, most countries with a sovereign currency also practise a floating exchange rate. Hereby, these countries get extra flexibility with regard to ironing out a deficit (or surplus) of foreign exchange. An imbalance in the market for foreign exchange will disappear when demand and supply make the exchange rate go down (or up) by market forces until equilibrium is established. Usually, it just means minor changes in the exchange rate to secure a balance between demand and supply. But, in cases like Brexit, the exchange rate suddenly can drop by nearly 10 % to establish a new equilibrium due to a brief but massive deficit at the capital account.

In rare cases where a country with a sovereign currency chooses to follow a fixed exchange rate policy, the central bank is committed to intervening in the foreign exchange market to secure that demand and supply in the foreign exchange market do equalise. Instead of letting the exchange rate adjust, the central bank needs to have a pile of foreign exchange in its 'cellar' for intervention whenever there is a lack of foreign exchange in the market. The Danish governments have chosen a fixed exchange rate policy in relation to the Euro. Hereby the Danish central bank has been forced to subordinate its monetary policy to the aim of keeping the exchange rate fixed. As a consequence, the central bank has to adjust its monetary policy in accordance with the surplus/deficit at the combined current and capital accounts. Hence, a (small) EU country following a fixed exchange rate policy towards the Euro has no monetary policy independence with regard to real sector activities, inflation and asset bubbles control. What is gained with respect to exchange rate stability is lost with regard to independent monetary policy unless the country takes up external capital controls.

Within a monetary union, the situation with regard to a combined deficit on the current and capital account is quite similar to the Danish case, except that Euro countries have no independent central bank. When borrowing in foreign private banks ceases and access to the European capital market dries up, which happened for a number of Euro countries during the crisis of 2010–2012, they have to rely on credit facilities within the ECB and other EU institutions. The conditions for the use of these facilities are decided case by case through a 'letter of understanding'. In the cases of Greece and Cyprus, while negotiations were dragging along, the private banking systems were literally for a while running dry of euro-notes. So, the withdrawal of deposits was limited in amount and capital control imposed. The national banking system of these two countries could not start working properly until an 'understanding' with the Euro institutions was 'agreed'.

These cases demonstrate that a surplus in the balance of payments is crucial when a country has given up monetary sovereignty; otherwise there is a risk of losing even more political sovereignty.

Monetary and Financial Instability Within the EMU

There is a trade-off between exchange rate stability and monetary policy independence for the Eurozone as a whole at the world exchange market. The ECB has chosen in collaboration with Brussels to let the euro exchange rate be (very) flexible (see Fig. 7.1). For instance, during a period of 5 years from 2000 to 2005 when euro-optimism was at its height, the currency's value against the dollar nearly doubled, which was extra harmful to the weakest Euro members. Finally, when the ECB started its quantitative easing programme in early 2015, the exchange rate dropped not dramatically, but at least it was back to a value similar to the one at the very beginning of the Eurozone in 1999, of 1.17 dollar/euro exchange rate.

The Dollar/Euro Exchange Rate – Instability

Sovereign countries, being members of a monetary union, are, except for the Eurozone, rare cases. Usually, a monetary union consists of a relatively large country (the mother country) with some minor semi-independent satellites, in combination with a kind of federal status. The EMU is a very special case. Participating countries have given up their national currency, that is, lost control of monetary and exchange rate policies without obtaining any federal commitment to compensate for this loss of sovereignty. Hence, the monetary policy of the entire union is at the discretion of the ECB, which is committed to act independently of the political system of Brussels and primarily to secure (consumer) price stability.

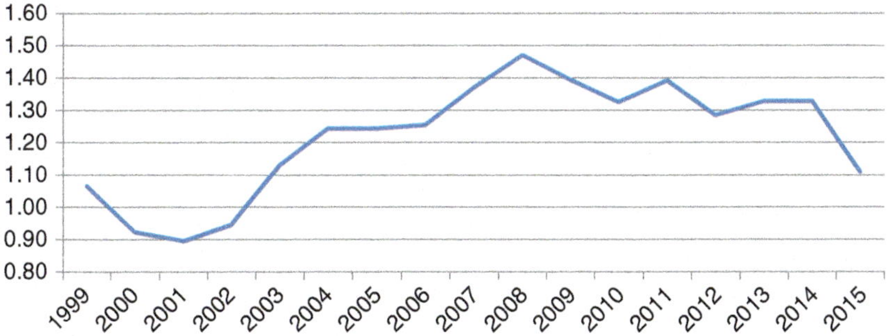

Fig. 7.1 The dollar/euro exchange rate

Source: European Central Bank (2016). http://www.ecb.europa.eu/stats/keyind/html/index.en.html

The EMU is an incomplete institutional monetary system; see De Grauwe (2016). It is notably exposed to financial imbalances caused by external events. The balance of payments (current and capital account) mirrors the monetary flows in and out of the country. A balance-of-payments deficit means the loss of liquidity, that is, a drain on money supply, which cannot be compensated by the government of a member country because the Euro countries have given up their independent central bank and, in doing so, their legal right to print money.

Within the Eurozone, the functioning of the monetary union depends on the size of balance-of-payments imbalances and the cross-border recycling mechanisms of liquidity. That is the ability, willingness and legal right of the ECB to act as lender of last resort, that is, to provide liquidity to (solvent) private banks in deficit countries. Until the financial crisis broke out in 2008, there was little need for the ECB to act as lender of last resort because private banks in the surplus countries (especially Germany and France) were more than willing to re-circulate their financial excess to southern Europe (and Ireland). In fact, the inter-bank risk premium was at a historical minimum in 2007 and banks did not see the financial shipwreck coming. Hence, current account deficits within the Eurozone were financed without difficulty.

The private banking sector could provide nearly limitless liquidity via the intra-Eurozone inter-bank market. One might wonder why the ECB did not worry about a money supply growing by 10 % or even more from 2003 onwards; see Fig. 7.2. But the ECB was, according to Euro-monetarist theory, only looking at the development in price inflation. The Eurozone excess of liquidity made it fairly easy to finance balance-of-payments deficit, housing bubbles and public sector deficits. There were no effective financial constrains undertaken by the ECB, which iterated 'we see no inflation'. Private banks in countries with a balance-of-payments surplus brought limitless quantities of southern European public sector bonds to get a slim extra. Before the financial crisis, these bonds were considered even by the international credit rating bureaus as risk-free and given a triple A rating! In countries with a balance-of-payments deficit, private banks could re-finance their liquidity deficit by borrowing either from private banks in surplus countries, that is, Germany, France and the Netherlands, or directly from the ECB system.

In 2003–2007, one can see that the financial sector – nicknamed 'the markets' – considered all Euro government bonds as being very close substitutes to German bonds, even the Greek bonds. This market process

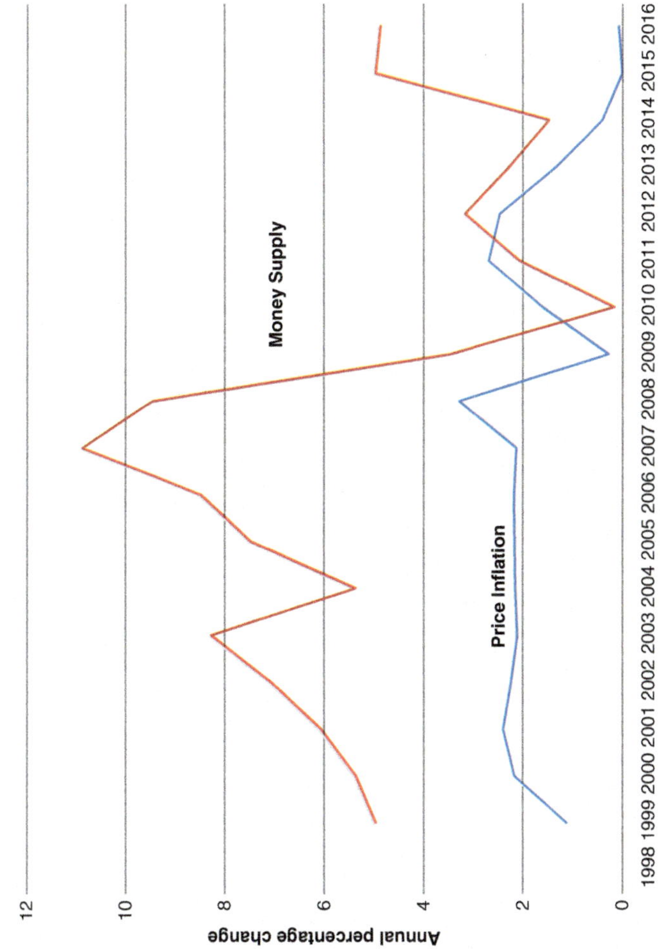

Fig. 7.2 Monetary instability and price inflation

Source: Eurostat, European Central Bank (2016). http://www.ecb.europa.eu/stats/keyind/html/index.en.html

is presented in the academic literature as representing a super rational actor coordinating savings and real investments via the ‘efficient market mechanism’, see for instance Fama (1970). According to this theory, no one can make better judgements than the ‘free’ and globalised markets on the ‘true’ value of financial assets.

Today, looking at what has happened during the past 10 years, it is hard to believe that all government bonds were considered as risk-free by the entire banking sector. However, numbers tell you that they were indeed so; all Eurozone government bonds were traded at a rate of interest with a spread to the German bonds of less than ½ percentage points. One really needs a microscope to see within this period any difference between the rates of interest of 10-year government bonds within the Eurozone.[2] The ‘markets’ had seemingly not understood that a common currency did not mean that all bonds had become as risk-free as German bonds. How could the different debtor risks be overlooked? The risk is – as we all know today – related to (1) currency, (2) asset price and finally (3) default (insolvency). Perhaps it would be more telling to name the phenomena ‘uncertainties’. The reason why the ‘markets’ had ‘overlooked’ such important uncertainties could be that, in the monetarist theory, there is no way to calculate uncertainty, that is, incorporate it into the mathematical model.

A more conspicuous explanation could be related to moral hazard. An assumption adopted by the main financial actors (i.e. the ‘market’) is, that if a perfect storm hits the financial markets in one country, then the government will step in and bail out the distressed financial institutions. In fact, this was what happened in 2008/2009, first in countries with a severe balance-of-payments deficit, such as Greece, Portugal and shortly after in Ireland. But in these Euro countries, without a printing press available, governments had to realise that they did not have enough liquidity to re-capitalise the troubled private banks and to cover their mounting budget deficit at the very same time. Hence, they had to go begging to the EU. This development was a clear manifestation of the difference made when a sovereign country had given up its constitutional right to print its own money. In contrast, the USA and UK did bail out some of their major banks (and insurance companies) using their national currency without being short of liquidity.

After an eruptive period from 2010 to 2012, where Euro institutions were in severe disarray with regard to financial market and bank support in the Eurozone countries, the long-term rates of interest have converged, except for Greece. After 2012, see Fig. 7.3.

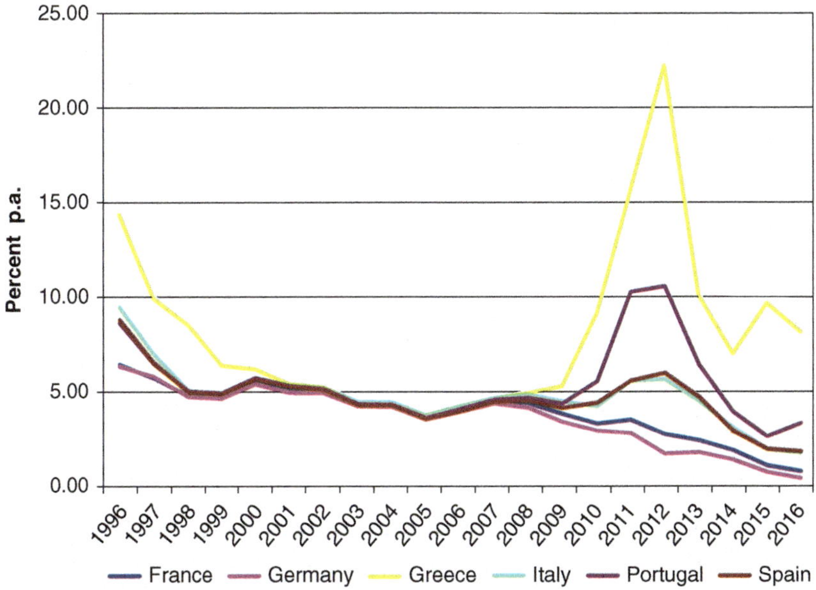

Fig. 7.3 Long term rate of interest, Euro-countries

Source: OECD, Economic Outlook, 2016/1

This convergence is by many observers mainly attributed to the appointment of Mario Draghi as ECB governor in the summer of 2012. He managed to get a broader mandate for financial market intervention and private bank liquidity support. His argument was that the ECB should do whatever was needed to 'save the euro' with regard to financial sector stability. The ECB made itself the lender of last resort and the ultimate buyer of government bonds in secondary markets. However, financially distressed governments had to sign a 'letter of understanding' before the ECB was prepared to exercise its unlimited support, which in fact did calm down speculation considerably.

A second institutional change was the establishment of a Eurozone borrowing facility for financially distressed governments. Originally the EU Treaty had a paragraph explicitly forbidding EU institutions (like the ECB or EIB) from supporting member states financially. However, when

Greece was denied access to the capital markets in 2010, the increased pressure on other weak Eurozone members made the financial system tremble and the common currency at risk. Either the Greek government had to get an emergency loan or the government (together with a number of Greek banks) would be bankrupt and eventually forced to re-establish its own national currency and re-introduce capital control, that is, a Grexit. In reality, this rescue package of the Greek public finances was mainly used to save private banks in Germany and France from the effects of holding Greek and Portuguese financial assets. An amendment of the EU Treaty made it possible to set up the ESM fund with a lending capacity of a €500 bill. As mentioned in 2012, the speculators on financial markets did calm down, thanks to the renewed mandate for ECB intervention. However, nothing shall be taken for granted in the future because, if a Euro-member government should need support, it still has to be evaluated by 'The Institutions' consisting of EU Commission, ECB and the IMF (formerly called the Troika).

These changes have made the Eurozone more prepared to resist a new financial crisis. Right now €100 billion have already been borrowed from the ESM fund. Time will tell the extent to which the remaining € 400 bill, together with the ECB initiatives, serves as a satisfactory bulwark. One may be doubtful because the previous crisis has required lending from the EU funds of more than €500 bill (see https://en.wikipedia.org/wiki/European_Stability_Mechanism, 28 June 2016).

At the bottom line, one can conclude that a fully integrated bank sector or financial markets has not yet been established. Until a banking union with shared regulation and shared rescue mechanisms is established, deposits in German banks with the backing of the German government are to be preferred to Greek banks with a number of withdrawal restrictions and a deposit guarantee issued by a much weaker government. From this perspective, Euro deposits have different qualities depending on bank and nationality, which the Cypriotes also had to take account of in 2013, when their banks had to be re-capitalised.

Intra-EMU Payments: The Target2 System

So, a euro is not always a euro because banks have different characteristics depending on, where their headquarter is located, the financial strength of the home-country's government and regulatory principles that apply within the different countries. In any case, until the financial crisis emerged, the European inter-bank market worked almost completely without friction. Until 2008, balance-of-payments imbalances were seemingly recycled without difficulties via the European and the Transatlantic inter-bank markets. Short-term lending between banks was considered safe; that is, until the default of Lehman Brothers in September 2008. All at once, inter-bank lending became restricted and much more costly. Suddenly, it was considered a risky business, especially when crossing borders. Private banks in countries with a balance-of-payments surplus found it much safer to deposit their surpluses in the national branch of the ECB, even if the rate of interest was low and became negative in 2015.

Within the ECB system, each member state operates its inter-bank market via the national branch of the ECB, which administrates the liquidity according to principles decided by the board of directors in Frankfurt. Hence, the German liquidity surplus is showing up as deposits in the German branch of the ECB system (the former German Bundesbank). The emergence of the Eurozone inter-bank distrust can be read from the ECB statistics.[3] Within a few years, the German branch accumulated a creditor position of more than € 700 bill. The main counterparts were the Spanish and Italian branches of the ECB system, because Euro deposits were literarily leaking out of the Italian, Spanish and other southern European banks towards German banks, which deposited the excess liquidity in the German branch.

The main subject of criticism of this cross-border ECB recycling was the unlimited credit facilities made available to solvent private banks. The idea was to facilitate daily cross-border payments between indisputable safe banks. This 'inter-European Central Bank market', called Target2 system, was established in early 2008, which has an unlimited short-term debit clearing facility and provides solvent private banks with necessary foreign liquidity. When the private inter-bank market stopped functioning frictionless, it was heavily supported by a clearing facility established via the ECB system. Before this moment, it had been the German, Dutch and French private banks which ran the major creditor risk. After 2008, fresh liquidity was provided by the central bank system. In the following figure, one can see how the accumulating balance-of-payments surpluses and deficits appeared in the ECB branch statistics.

However, a hang-over of debt from the 'old' balance-of-payments deficits derived before 2008 due to current account deficits in Greece, Spain and Portugal were still on the books of the private banks in the surplus countries. This existing *foreign* debt was partly guaranteed and partly taken over by the national governments from banks going bust.

From 2008, the public finance of the weaker Eurozone members experienced a double liquidity squeeze. The public sector current deficit had enlarged and governments had taken over a huge amount of private banks' liabilities with bad assets, creating an immense financial need. This mess over the public sector budget caused credit rating bureaus to downgrade government debt, which caused the interest rate to rise rapidly and made it nearly impossible for these governments to sell bonds on the conventional markets. As we have explained before, the EU stepped in first at an inter-governmental level because the EU Treaty did not allow EU institutions to finance broken governments. The situation changed after 2012 when ECB started to buy private and later government bonds in the secondary markets, while the EU Treaty was amended to allow loans directly to distressed member countries from an EU institution.

Amongst other critics, Sinn (2012) has been very critical towards the semi-automatic recycling of liquidity from surplus countries to deficit countries within the ECB system. He views this recycling as leading to a kind of moral hazard, where running a balance-of-payments deficit could go unquestioned for much too long and thereby cause a threat to Germany's financial stability, if the process of breaking up the Eurozone gained momentum. His fear in 2012–2013 was that a sudden collapse of the common currency and the ECB system would leave the German Bundesbank with a huge amount of nearly valueless claims on the southern European banks. His main arguments are directed towards the much too easy recycling of liquidity back to countries with a balance-of-payments deficit. This recycling took away any immediate incentive to reduce these deficits, that is, according to his monetarist theory, to improve competitiveness by wage reduction and reduce public sector deficit.

But Sinn's arguments are somewhat flawed. First, one could argue that if the balance-of-payments surplus makes the Germany financial sector more fragile, then an obvious policy would be to reduce this surplus to the benefit of the German citizens and the unemployed people in southern Europe. Second, liquidity provided by the ECB system might not in the future be limitless. So, the Euro member states have to remove their balance-of-payments deficits to stop borrowing abroad. Or thirdly, see Fig. 7.4 if the surplus countries are unwilling to reduce their surpluses, the Eurozone as a whole had to create a substantial external surplus, which would be large enough to give all the Eurozone countries a balance-of-payments surplus. A combination of

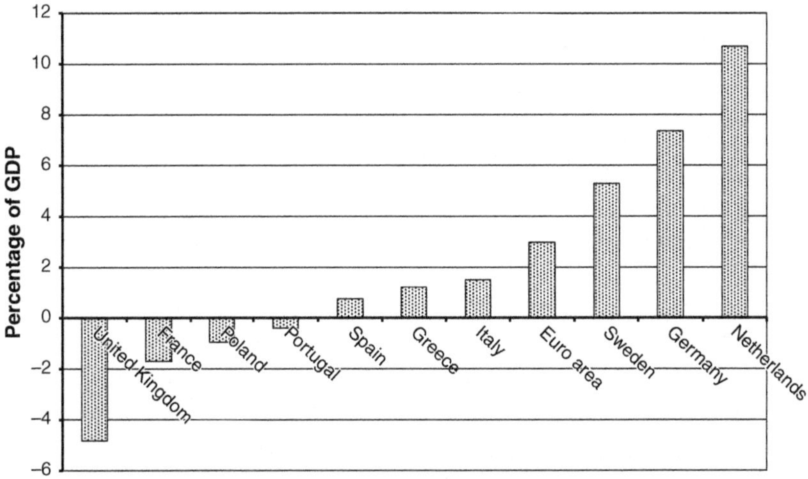

Fig. 7.4 Balance of Payments, current account, 2014

Source: OECD, Economic Outlook, 2016

austerity policy, wage reduction and euro depreciation paved the way for such a huge Eurozone surplus, but at the expense of economic stagnation, falling wage shares and increased social misery, see Chap. 6.

Some Concluding Remarks on Eurozone Financial Instability

I feel tempted to call the monetary and financial part of the Maastricht Treaty as 'mission impossible'. The ECB is required to secure consumer price stability within the Eurozone, consisting of nineteen separate economies. The monetary policy undertaken in the first 10 years has become a compromise between a German economy being in semi-recession and the booming southern European countries. ECB could not prevent the cost levels from continuing to diverge, causing increasing balance-of-payment surpluses and deficits. These imbalances were financed through the European inter-bank market, seemingly without any difficulty until it came to a sudden stop in 2008.

In the wake of the international bank and finance crises, it became obvious that European banks were shaky and some did collapse. However, governments within the Eurozone had difficulties to re-capitalise the national banking system without being supported with liquidity from the ECB system or the special EU euro fund, in regard to which some delay has occurred.

Broadly speaking, one can conclude that the liquidity-squeezed Eurozone countries were very badly prepared to withstand the financial crisis and that they received very little real support from the surplus countries. The main interest of surplus countries was to rescue their own private banking system by lifting southern European loans from the books of private banks to the newly established euro funds. In this sense, no taxpayers' money has been immediately involved, only government guarantees until now. However, southern Europe governments have become burdened by this bank debt and been forced by creditors to follow a restrictive fiscal policy, which has made these countries experience an economic depression not seen since the 1930s.

In broad terms, all the non-Eurozone countries did somewhat better than the average of the Eurozone. Unemployment did not rise to anything close to the Eurozone level, neither as an average nor in any individual country. The main reason for their 'softer landing' after the 2008 recession was the exchange rate and monetary policies which were undertaken by the non-Euro countries. None of the governments was 'liquidity-squeezed', because they had their own national printing press. They could let the value of the national currency fall if necessary, in order to regain international competitiveness. Hence, they started quantitative easing and zero-rate interest policies years long before the ECB. So, the non-Euro countries had much more leeway with regard to economic policies to counter-weigh the private excess savings and hereby been less distressed by unemployment and/or balance-of-payments deficit.

This is a lesson to keep in mind and to learn from before the next crisis hits the EU.

Notes

1. Title of a path-breaking post-Keynesian book by Paul Davidson back in 1973
2. Slovakia did not become member of the Eurozone until 2009
3. See Euro Crisis Monitor, Institute of Empirical Economic Research, Osnabrück University Data source: European Central Bank

CHAPTER 8

Any Future of the Euro?

Abstract The EMU in its present form has come to a dead end. Stagnation, high unemployment and huge balance-of-payments surpluses cannot go on. Macroeconomic imbalances and popular discontent accumulate. If a future dissolution similar to the Gold Standard in the1930s should be avoided, a much needed Solidarity Fond has to be set-up. Countries with balance-of-payments surplus above 3 percent and foreign wealth beyond 60 percent of GDP should deposit the excess without interest. The revenue could be used to improve productivity in backward regions of deficit countries. In addition, public finances should no longer be a EU concern, but left to the national governments to decide upon.

According to many Euro-realists, the EMU was – and still is – much too prematurely established. The Euro could be kept only as a parallel currency valued as a weighted average of all EU national currencies somewhat similar to the ECU, which worked quite well before the EMU was established.

Keywords Euro-realism · Re-design of EMU · Solidarity Fond · Ceiling of balance-of-payments surplus · Re-nationalised currencies · Euro as a parallel currency

The Past

The argument of this book is that the Euro or, more precisely, the EMU has failed. This is a proposition that is difficult to disagree with from a macroeconomic viewpoint. What we have witnessed in the southern

J. Jespersen, *The Euro*, DOI 10.1007/978-3-319-46388-9_8

European Euro-countries is a macroeconomic imbalance not seen since the 1930s. From a historical perspective, there are a number of similarities between the Great Depression and this 'great recession' that we are living through right now. The calamities of the 1930s did occur with a background of a mismanaged international monetary system. This period is usually called the era of the International Gold Standard, which lasted from 1925 to 1931/1936.[1]

There seem to be many similarities to the EMU, but, of course, 80 years of time and a World War have changed many institutions, policies and macroeconomic insights. One important difference is that the common currency, the euro, is used as means of payments in each Eurozone country. In the inter-war period, gold coins were hardly used in the private sector, where national currencies, although anchored to a fixed gold exchange rate, circulated. Hence, one should be careful to draw too firm a parallel between then and now.

On the other hand, one important conclusion we have drawn across these chapters is that the dominating macroeconomic arguments and policy conclusions are strikingly similar to the 1930s. Although Maynard Keynes's macroeconomics emerged from the unemployment crisis of the 1930s, they were not referred to when the EMU was discussed and institutionalised in the early years of the 1990s. Similarly, no one paid much consideration to Keynes's suggestions for a new international monetary system lying behind the Bretton Woods agreement in 1944. This was a mistake. Deeper insights were omitted and a half-baked monetary union was established.

We judge the EMU to be half-baked because it has only focused on national public sector imbalances and on inflation, without consideration for unemployment and the balance of payments. Hence, national policies have presently primarily been focused on balancing the public budget independent of other macroeconomic imbalances. Furthermore, the monetary policy of the ECB was directed towards price stability measured by an average of the development of the participating countries.

The underlying macroeconomic theory of the EMU was inspired by monetarism, but of a special kind, where exchange rates were kept fixed and unchangeable due to the common currency. According to this macroeconomic theory model, it was assumed that market forces would secure the needed adjustments to create an Optimal Currency Area within the Eurozone. In the theoretical textbooks and using a mathematical simulation model, this adjustment process seemed to go on quite well. It was believed to take some time to adjust, but through time the national economies were assumed to become more and more flexible and similar. Hence, the policy conclusion reached by the Euro-monetarists was that it would be quite likely that the Eurozone could develop into an Optimal Currency Area, within a relatively short period to the benefit of all participating countries, and that the mistakes of the Gold Standard could be avoided – see, for instance, Sørensen (2005).

The Present

Obviously, something was wrong. The euro system was not to the benefit of all the participating countries. Growth rates for the Eurozone as a whole became weak and very unevenly distributed among the member countries. Unemployment went up and even more unevenly distributed among the member countries; a development rather different from that of the non-Euro countries, which had kept its monetary sovereignty. The crisis had unveiled, how much more difficult it had become for the Eurozone countries to navigate through a sea of macroeconomic imbalances.

These countries came to realise that giving up monetary sovereignty was a major problem for countries running a substantial balance-of-payments deficit. The time the crisis hit, they had built up a large foreign debt. These countries experienced when the European inter-bank market froze, a severe liquidity squeeze. Without command over a national currency and monetary policy, these countries found themselves at the mercy of the credit rating bureaus and of the European/international capital markets. Many private debtors went bankrupt. Private banks came to realise that they had mis-judged the risk related to foreign lending and that many loans would never be paid back. Hence, national governments had to support their domestic banking system, which was expensive in any case; but especially difficult for the liquidity-squeezed Eurozone countries with balance-of-payments deficit and no access to the printing press.

Those governments, which were denied access to the European financial markets at reasonable terms, had to declare themselves in a state of financial emergency. A situation arose which could only be solved either by the country leaving the euro system and reintroducing a national currency or to ask the other Eurozone members and the Euro institutions for an extraordinary financial support. Greece was the first country to ask for such a Eurozone loan. However, Portugal, Ireland and Cyprus followed shortly after, while Spain got a special arrangement later for the re-capitalisation of their banks.

Conditions for these emergency loans were dictated by the so-called Troika (EU Commission, ECB and IMF), which subscribed to the Euro-monetarist way of thinking. Therefore, these loans were conditioned on an agreed (i.e. dictated) plan for how to re-establish a balanced public sector budget, independently of how the real activity and unemployment developed. With the exception of Ireland, there has been hardly any real growth in these countries since they received these emergency loans. Instead, unemployment is still at a high level and poverty is growing.

This is why the Euro has failed. Its institutional arrangements have created a structural straitjacket of a kind that has prevented the most disadvantaged economies from improving their lot using national policy instruments. In setting up a monetary union, it should had been emphasised that the balance of payments is the most important link between the participating countries. Therefore, the institutional framework should primarily have put limits on the size of the accepted deficits and surpluses at the current account. A surplus is causing stress on the trading partners and undermines the financial stability of the deficit countries. After 17 years of growing real economic divergence between surplus and deficit countries, the Eurozone is further away from the definition of an Optimal Currency Area than ever. This unstable situation has to be understood, and to be acted upon quickly, before the socially deprived people more definitively abandon the idea of the EMU as a mutually beneficial project with a shared prosperity for all participants.

The Future?

The present situation is the outcome of a neo-functionalistic approach to European integration. The founding fathers of the EMU knew that the euro system was not perfect, but they saw the common currency as a useful vehicle to create a common European identity. Later on, when difficulties arose, it was expected by the neo-functionalists, who were dominated by Euro-monetarist thinking that there hereby would be a call for a closer cooperation within the Eurozone. Heads of government would be asked to surrender more sovereignty to Brussels in the name of 'overcoming the crisis'.

Euro-monetarists have long argued for the need of a federal budget procedure to control rather than to coordinate public finances. The establishment of the Fiscal Compact, together with the European Semester, where national budgets for the coming year are controlled by the EU Commission, was a step in such a federal direction. One can see that the Euro-monetarists view public finance as the root cause of the malfunctioning of the EMU.

But, according to the empirical analysis put forward in this book, the underlying structural problems of the EMU will not be solved by the request of balancing the public budget. It is rather the substantial balance-of-payments surpluses (and related deficits) which caused frictions and instability to build up. Surplus countries accumulate more and more foreign assets, which gives them a dominant role as the creditor and, in reality, the paymaster of the EMU, who can decide on politics in debtor countries. This uneven development where creditor countries can dictate policies is running counter to the basic democratic idea of the EU and to the principle of subsidiarity, which is regarded as true European values and hence as cornerstones of European cooperation rather than forced integration.

What would the *Euro-realist* argue, given the present situation? There are few joint and commonly shared arguments. A simple, but politically difficult suggestion would be to dissolve the monetary union. To give back monetary sovereignty to those individual countries, which obviously were not ready to share a common currency, when economic structures and aspirations were – and still are – so different. Yet, the dilemma of southern Europe cannot be solved by this simple solution, because a majority of the populations in these countries are pleased with the euro as a means of payments, although very dissatisfied with the macroeconomic consequences in terms of unemployment, foreign indebtedness and a loss of sovereignty. Hence, in these countries, the euro could be used as a parallel currency, which firms and households could use to settle contracts. But they should be aware that the exchange rate between the national currency and the euro could change.

An even more radical idea is to re-establish the pre-EMU European accountant unit at that time called an ECU and let it be the parallel currency and legal tender in all EU countries. Let us instead call it a 'EUnit'. The value of the EUnit should be defined as a weighted average of all EU currencies: (1) countries which have kept its own currency, (2) Euro countries which have re-nationalised their old currency and (3) Euro countries which have kept the 'old' Euro. Brussels should be forced to use the EUnit as the unit of account, means of payments and when intervention prices are set in, for instance, the Common Agricultural Policies.

In any case, the main argument of this book is the unsolved problem of persistent balance-of-payments surpluses (and deficits), which is only partly addressed by the proposed re-nationalisation of the currency in (some of) the Eurozone countries. There has to be built into the 'Stability Pact' a firm commitment not to run balance-of-payments surpluses above, for instance, 3 percent of GDP and no foreign wealth exceeding say 60 percent (of course, these numbers should not be arbitrarily chosen, like the numbers in the Stability Pact related to public finances are today). In fact, these numbers related to the balance of payments should be discussed with reference to the level of cross-border transactions within the EU and supported with institutional arrangements to correct such imbalances in a mutually respectful way. But also with a view at the global economic, where reduced balance-of-payments imbalances also would be preferable, although they can more easily be corrected via exchange rate adjustments.

At this stage one should recall or re-read Maynard Keynes's proposal at the Bretton Woods conference back in 1944, where he suggested that surplus countries should be required to make a deposit into an International clearing bank of any amount exceeding an agreed ceiling. These revenues should eventually flow into the most distressed regions of the deficit countries. Today, such an arrangement with a European clearing bank would give a much needed incentive to the government of surplus countries to make a domestic fiscal expansion, which would reduce the surplus and be to the benefit of all parties at home and abroad. Today the Germans would probably fiercely resist the idea of a European clearing bank. Back in 1944 the Americans opposed Keynes's suggested surplus procedure, but shortly after they had to realise that a substantial transfer to Europe (the deficit region) was needed, and the Marshall Aid was organised. A re-designed Stability Pact, where surplus countries are requested to transfer parts of their excess money, would not only stabilise the EMU but also add a much needed element of solidarity to the working of the EU. On the other hand, the deficit countries should be required to improve on their current account by increasing their international competitiveness. As we know, competitiveness is a matter of improved productivity and relative cost levels. The preference should be on improving productivity rather than on reducing wage cost. But deficit countries do not have to be threatened by being fined. They already feel the pain of the deficit by paying interest on their foreign debt and by having lost jobs due to the negative trade balance.

To be realistic about what could be expected to happen in Europe in the coming years, one has to turn the attention towards Germany and France, especially, when the United Kingdom has voted to leave the EU. One important question is, to what extent Germany will accept her European responsibility, like the Americans did after the Second World War. If one could imagine Germany showing the same kind of solidarity with the distressed regions, then a sea-change in favour of pro-European sentiment could be re-gained in Europe. But, where is France going? Will she accept to play the second violin after Germany, or will she follow Marine le Pen on a nationalist agenda, which probably means a withdrawal from the monetary union? If so, the euro will cease to exist.

Let me conclude by saying, that one has to regret that the euro was launched prematurely. However, it is a fact that many Europeans do appreciate the euro as a stable means of payments. But a popular resistance against further centralism is building up in many EU countries also outside the Eurozone. More and more people understand that they have been mis-led by the Euro-monetarist arguments and the neo-functionalist strategy. In fact, the social costs had in some regions become unbearably high, which leaves people in despair and disillusion with regard to European integration.

So, what is to be done? My best answer is that those countries that have benefited the most should generously compensate the deficit countries. Not necessarily without commitments, but organised in such a way that the European people stop turning their back to European-initiated solutions, because the EMU has to be re-designed profoundly within a short while, if the fate, which befell the Gold Standard in the 1930s, should be avoided.

Note

1. UK left the Gold Standard in 1931, France not until 1936, see Eichengreen 1996/1998

Bibliography

Best, H., Lengyel, G., & Verzichelli, L. (Eds.). (2012). *The Europe of elites*. Oxford: Oxford University Press.

Bibow, J. (2012). *The Euro debt crisis and Germany's Euro trilemma*. Working Paper No. 721 Levy Economics Institute of Bard College May.

Chang, M. (2009). *Monetary integration in the European Union*. London: Palgrave Macmillan.

Clower, R. (1965). The Keynesian counter-revolution: A theoretical appraisal. In F. H. Hahn and F. P. R. Brechling (Eds.), *The theory of interest rates*. London: Macmillan.

Davidson, P. (1973). *Money and the real world*. London: Macmillan.

Davidson, P. (2009). *The Keynes solution: The path to global economic prosperity*. London: Palgrave Macmillan.

De Grauwe, P. (1999). Risks of a roofless Euroland. *Time Magazine*, January 11.

De Grauwe, P. (2016). *Economics of monetary union* (11th edn.). Oxford: Oxford University Press.

Delors Report (Committee for the Study of Economic and Monetary Union). (1989). *Report on economic and monetary union in the European community*. Luxemburg: Office for Official Publications of the EC.

Eichengreen, B. (1996/1998). *Globalizing capital: A history of the international monetary system*. Princeton: Princeton University Press.

EU-Commission. (1990, October). One market, one money. An evaluation of the potential benefits and costs of forming an economic and monetary union. *European Economy, 44*.

Fama, E. F. (1970). Efficient capital markets: A review of theory and empirical work. *The Journal of Finance, 25*(2), 383–417.

Forder J. (2014). *Macroeconomics and the Phillips curve myth*. Oxford: Oxford University Press.

J. Jespersen, *The Euro*, DOI 10.1007/978-3-319-46388-9

Frenkel, J., & Johnson, H. G. (eds.), (1976). *The monetary approach to the balance of payments* (pp. 262–284). Toronto: University of Toronto Press.

Friedman, M. (1969). *The optimal quantity of money and other essays.* Chicago: Aldine Publishing Company.

Glick, R., & Rose, A. K. (2015). *Currency unions and trade: A post-EMU mea culpa.* Federal Reserve Bank of San Francisco Working Paper 2015–11.

Guajardo, J., Leigh, D., & Pescatori, A. (2011). Expansionary austerity: New international evidence. IMF Working Paper WP/11/158. Washington, DC: International Monetary Fund.

Hebsgaard, T. (2011, January 6). Overvismand: 'Det dominerer jo også debatten, at vand fryser ved nul grader. *Information, article.*

Hoffmeyer, E. (2005). Den politiske historie om Den Økonomiske og Monetære union. Odense: Syddansk Universitetsforlag, 294.

Jespersen, J. (2009). *Macroeconomic methodology: A post-Keynesian perspective.* Cheltenham: Edward Elgar.

Jespersen, J. (2012). *The Euro: Why it went wrong and how to get on?* Copenhagen: DEO (in Danish).

Jespersen, J. (2013). *A European nightmare: How could it happen?* Churchill College Lecture. http://www.insightweb.it/web/files/a_european_nightmare.pdf

Jespersen, J. (2016). *Structural budget deficits: Getting causality right.* In Madsen, M. O., & Olesen, F. (Eds.), Macroeconomics after the financial crisis. London: Routledge.

Jespersen, J., & Jensen, H. R. (2013). *Introduction to macroeconomics.* Copenhagen: Djøfs Forlag(in Danish).

Johnson, H. G. (1977). The monetary approach to balance of payments theory and policy: Explanation and policy implications. *Economica, 44*(175) (August), 217–229.

Keynes, J. M. (1933). National self-sufficiency. *The Yale Review*, *22*(4) (June) 755–769.

Keynes, J. M. (1936). *The general theory of employment, interest and money.* London: Macmillan.

Lavoie, M., & Stockhammer, E. (2012). Wage-led growth: Concept, theories and policies. *Conditions of Work and Employment Series, No. 41*, Geneva: ILO.

Lechevalier, A., & Wielgohs, J. (eds). (2015). *Social Europe: A dead end: What the Eurozone crisis is doing to Europe's social dimension.* Copenhagen: DJØF Publishing.

Legrain, Ph. (2014). *European spring: Why our economies and politics are in a mess.* published by the author, distributed by Amazon.

Lucas, R. E., Jr. (1987). *Models of business cycles.* Oxford: Blackwell.

Lucas, R. E., Jr., & Sargent, T. J. (1979). After Keynesian macroeconomics. *Quarterly Review*, Federal Reserve Bank of Minneapolis, Spring issue.

Madsen, M. O., & Olesen, F. (eds). (2016). *Macroeconomics after the financial crisis*. London: Routledge.

Majone, G. (2014). *Rethinking the union of Europe post-crisis: Has integration gone too far?* Cambridge, UK: Cambridge University Press.

Mankiw, G. N. (2016). *Macroeconomics*. 9th edn. New York: Worth Publishers.

Mundell, R. (1961, September). A theory of optimal currency areas. *American Economic Review*, *51*(4), 657–665.

OECD Economic Outlook No. 99 (Edition 2016/1), web-site: http://stats.oecd.org/BrandedView.aspx?oecd_bv_id=eo-data-en&doi=9572784d-en.

Ostry, J. D., Loungani, P., & Furceri, D. (2016). Neoliberalism, oversold? *Finance & Development (IMF)*, *53*(2) (June), pp. 38–41.

Patinkin, D. (1958). Liquidity preference and loanable funds: Stock and flow analysis. *Economica*, NS 25, 300–318.

Pew Research Center. (2015, June). *Faith in European project reviving*.

Rose, A. K. (2000). One money, one market: estimating the effect of common currencies on trade Economic Policy 2000; A non-technical version "Does a Currency Union Boost International Trade?" California Management Review 2000.

Rosser, J. R., Holt, R. R. F., & Colander, D. (2010). *European economics at a crossroad*. Cheltenham: Edward Elgar.

Sinn, Hans-Werner. (2012). *The Euro trap. On bursting bubbles, budgets, and beliefs*. Oxford: Oxford University Press.

Skott, P. (2016). *Public debt, secular stagnation and functional finance*. Madsen and Olesen (Eds). London: Routledge.

Sørensen, P. B. (ed.). (2005). *Monetary union in Europe: Historical perspectives and prospects for the future*. Copenhagen: DJØF Publishing.

Thirlwall, A. P. (ed.). (1976). *Keynes and international monetary relations*. London & Basingstoke: Macmillan.

Varoufakis, Y. (2016). *And the weak suffer what they must?: Europe, austerity and the threat to global stability*. London: The Bodley Head.

Wallace, P. (2016). *The €uro experiment*. Cambridge: Cambridge University Press.

Wilkinson, R., & Pickett, K. (2010). *The spirit level: Why equality is better for everyone*. London: Penguin Books.

Index

J. Jespersen, *The Euro*, DOI 10.1007/978-3-319-46388-9

CPSIA information can be obtained
at www.ICGtesting.com
Printed in the USA
LVOW05*2340171017
552830LV00017B/260/P

9 783319 463872